DELIRIUM'S PARTY

a little **ENDLESS** storybook

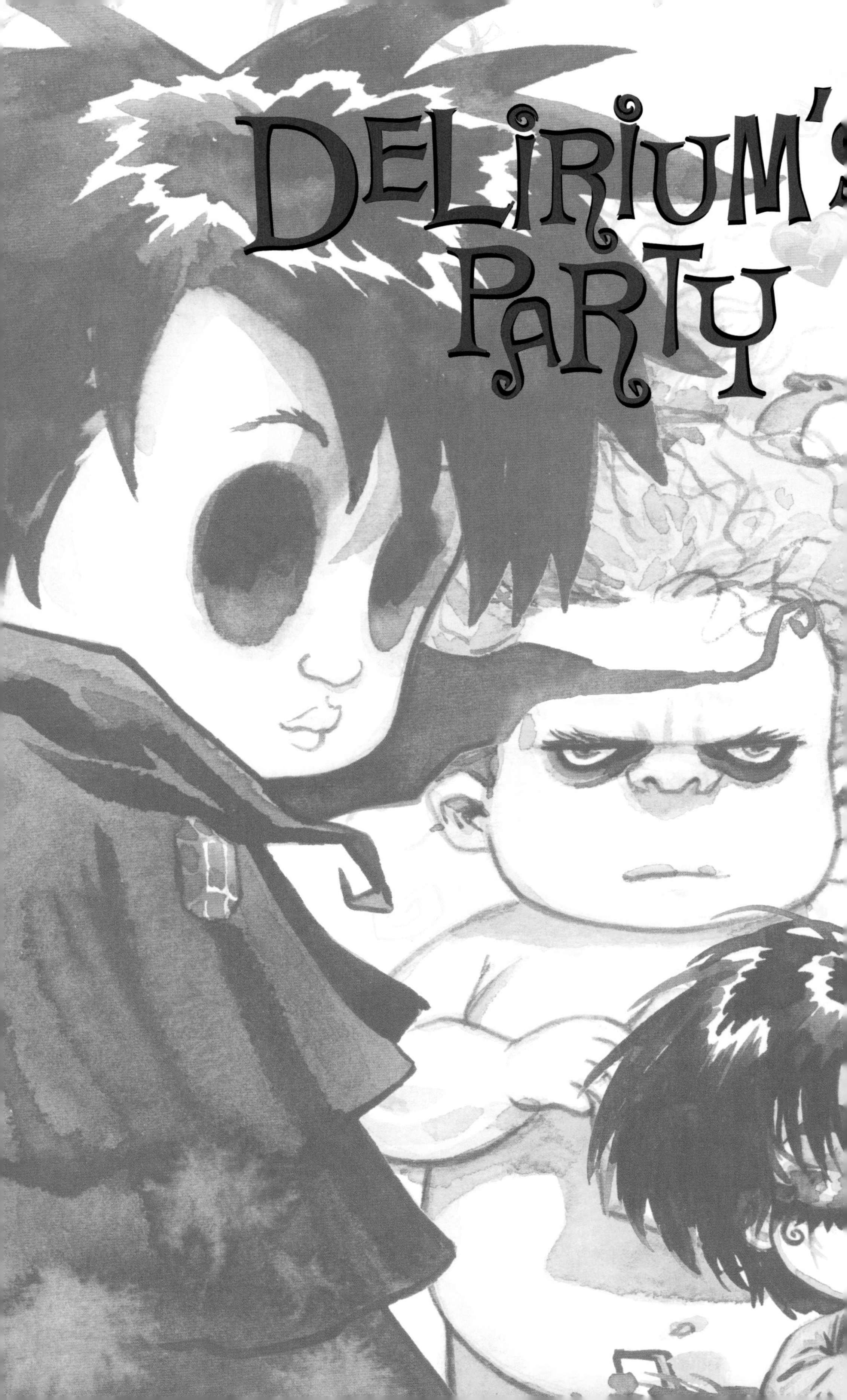
DELIRIUM'S
PARTY

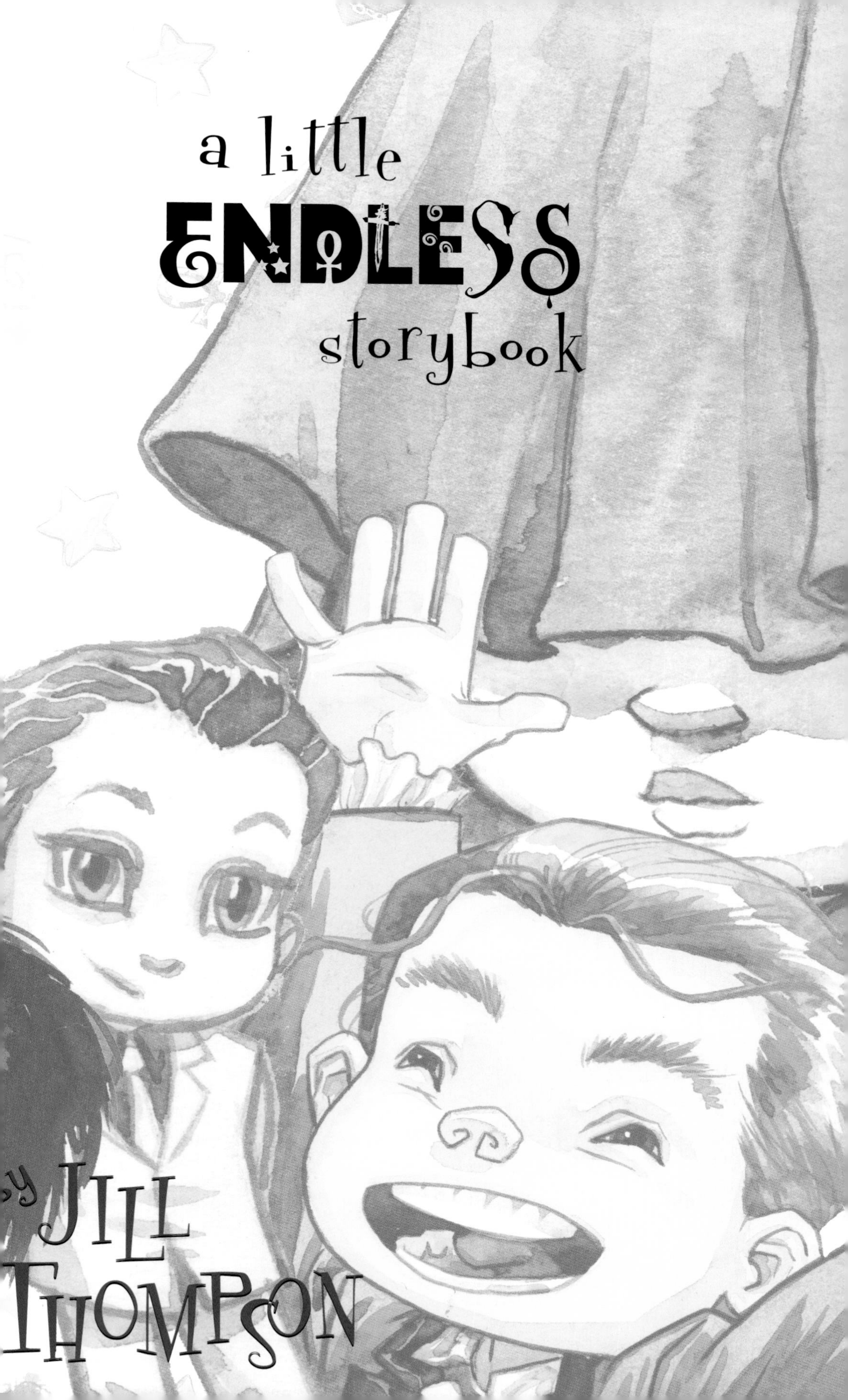
a little
ENDLESS
storybook
JILL
THOMPSON

Karen Berger SVP-Executive Editor
Shelly Bond Editor
Angela Rufino Associate Editor
Gregory Lockard Assistant Editor
Robbin Brosterman Design Director-Books
Curtis King Jr. Senior Art Director

DC COMICS

Diane Nelson President
Dan DiDio and Jim Lee Co-Publishers
Geoff Johns Chief Creative Officer
Patrick Caldon EVP-Finance and Administration
John Rood EVP-Sales, Marketing and Business Development
Amy Genkins SVP-Business and Legal Affairs
Steve Rotterdam SVP-Sales and Marketing
John Cunningham VP-Marketing
Terri Cunningham VP-Managing Editor
Alison Gill VP-Manufacturing
David Hyde VP-Publicity
Sue Pohja VP-Book Trade Sales
Alysse Soll VP-Advertising and Custom Publishing
Bob Wayne VP-Sales
Mark Chiarello Art Director

Neil Gaiman, consultant
Painted cover by Jill Thompson
Endless Logo Design by Nancy Ogami
Publication design by Amie Brockway-Metcalf

Photo of Jill Thompson by DANO.

The Sandman is created by Gaiman, Kieth and Dringenberg.

DELIRIUM'S PARTY:
A LITTLE ENDLESS STORYBOOK
Published by DC Comics, 1700 Broadway, New York, NY 10019.

Printed by RR Donnelley,
Willard, OH, USA (4/27/11). First Printing.
DC Comics, a Warner Bros. Entertainment Company.
HC ISBN: 978-1-4012-2477-6.
SC ISBN: 978-1-4012-2478-3.

SUSTAINABLE FORESTRY INITIATIVE
Certified Chain of Custody
Promoting Sustainable Forest Management
www.sfiprogram.org

Fiber used in this product line meets the sourcing requirements of the SFI program.
www.sfiprogram.org SGS-SFI/COC-US10/81072

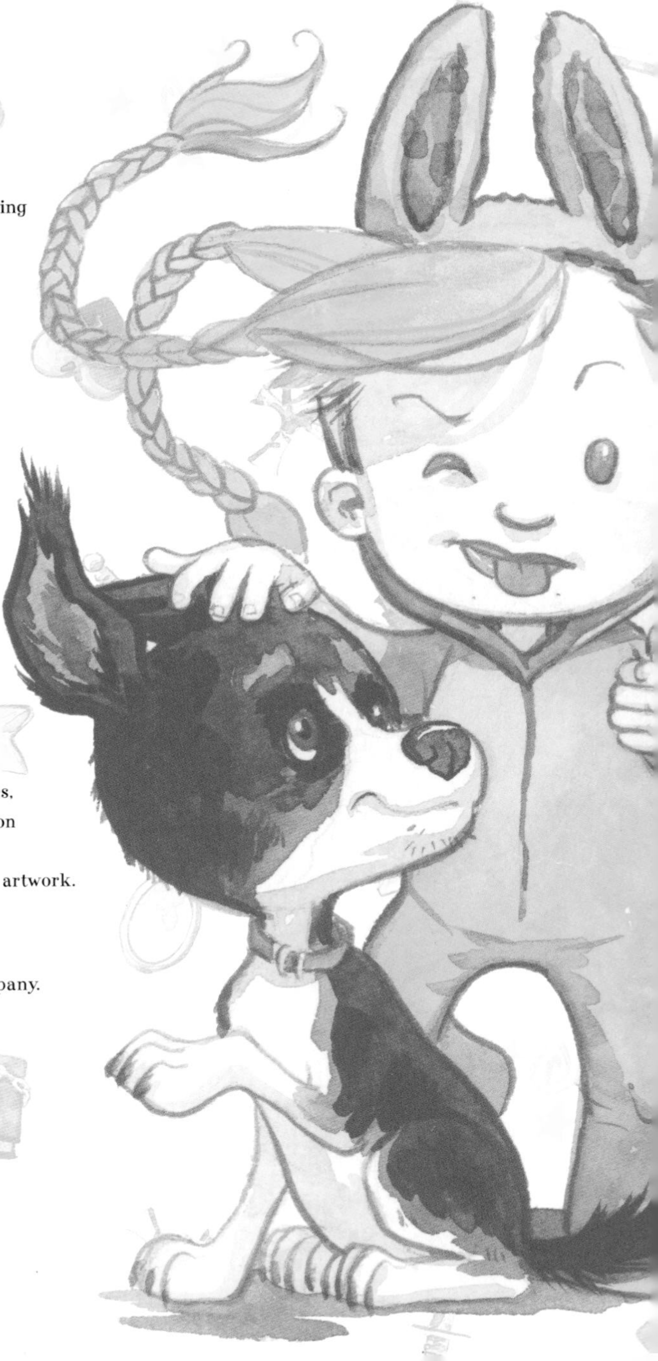

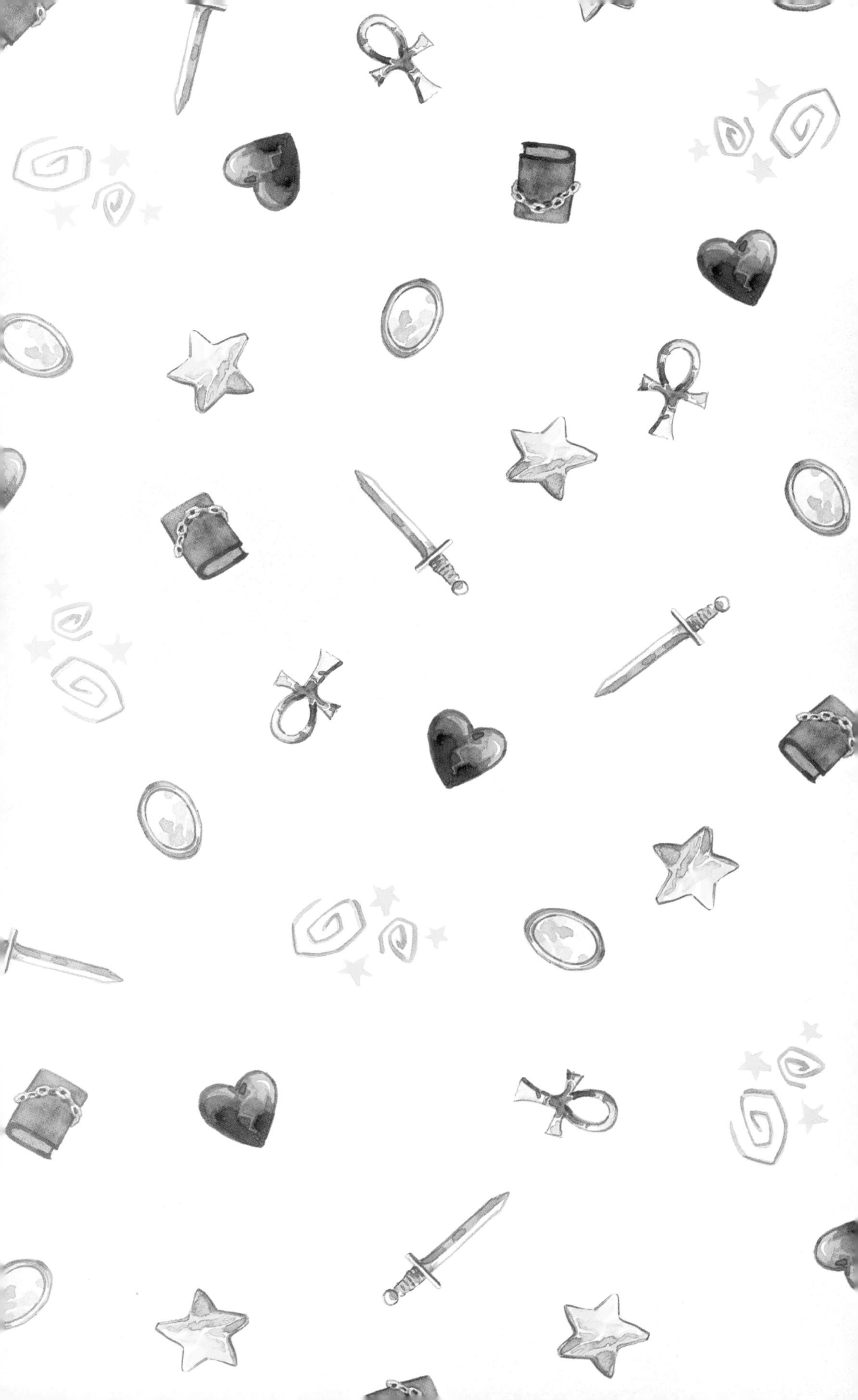

To Ella and Hollis — both of whom are the life of a party...

— *Jill Thompson*

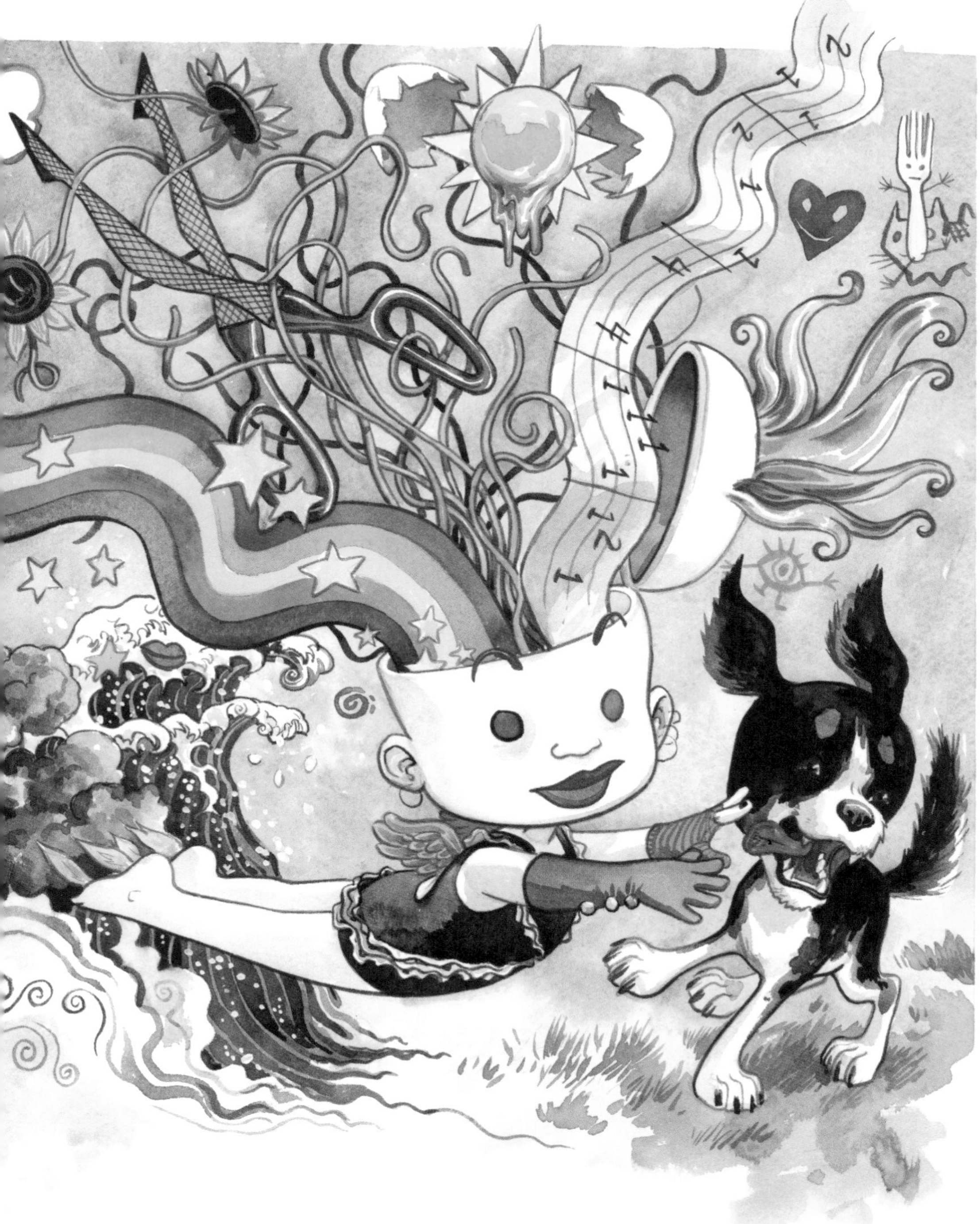

Once upon a time in the land of twinkles and sparks,
there lived a Princess named Delirium.
She had a fine companion named Barnabas
and a colorful realm to call her very own.
The Princess (and her doggie) spent the days
wandering among the people,
keeping things unpredictable and twirly.

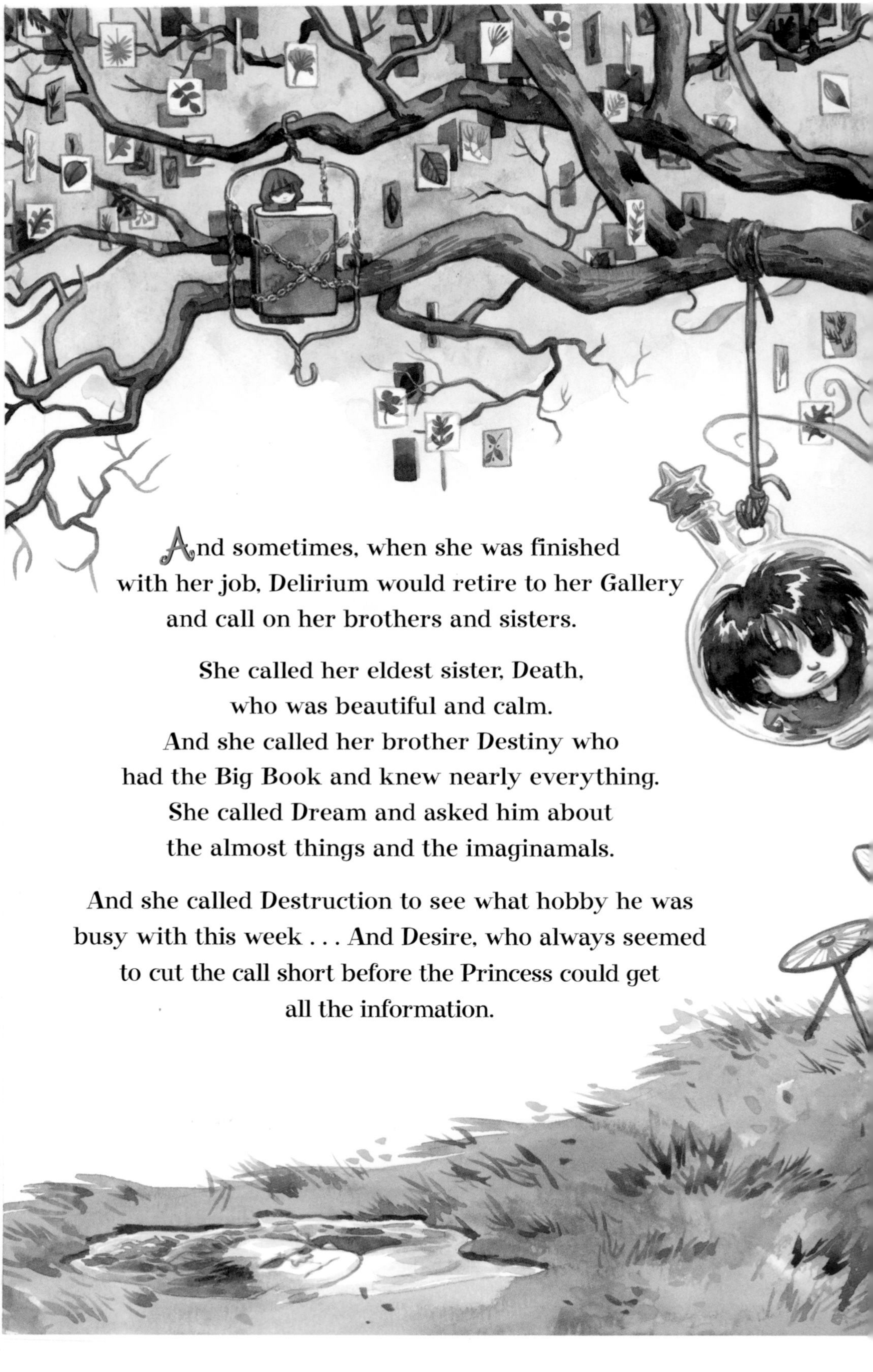

And sometimes, when she was finished with her job, Delirium would retire to her Gallery and call on her brothers and sisters.

She called her eldest sister, Death, who was beautiful and calm. And she called her brother Destiny who had the Big Book and knew nearly everything. She called Dream and asked him about the almost things and the imaginamals.

And she called Destruction to see what hobby he was busy with this week . . . And Desire, who always seemed to cut the call short before the Princess could get all the information.

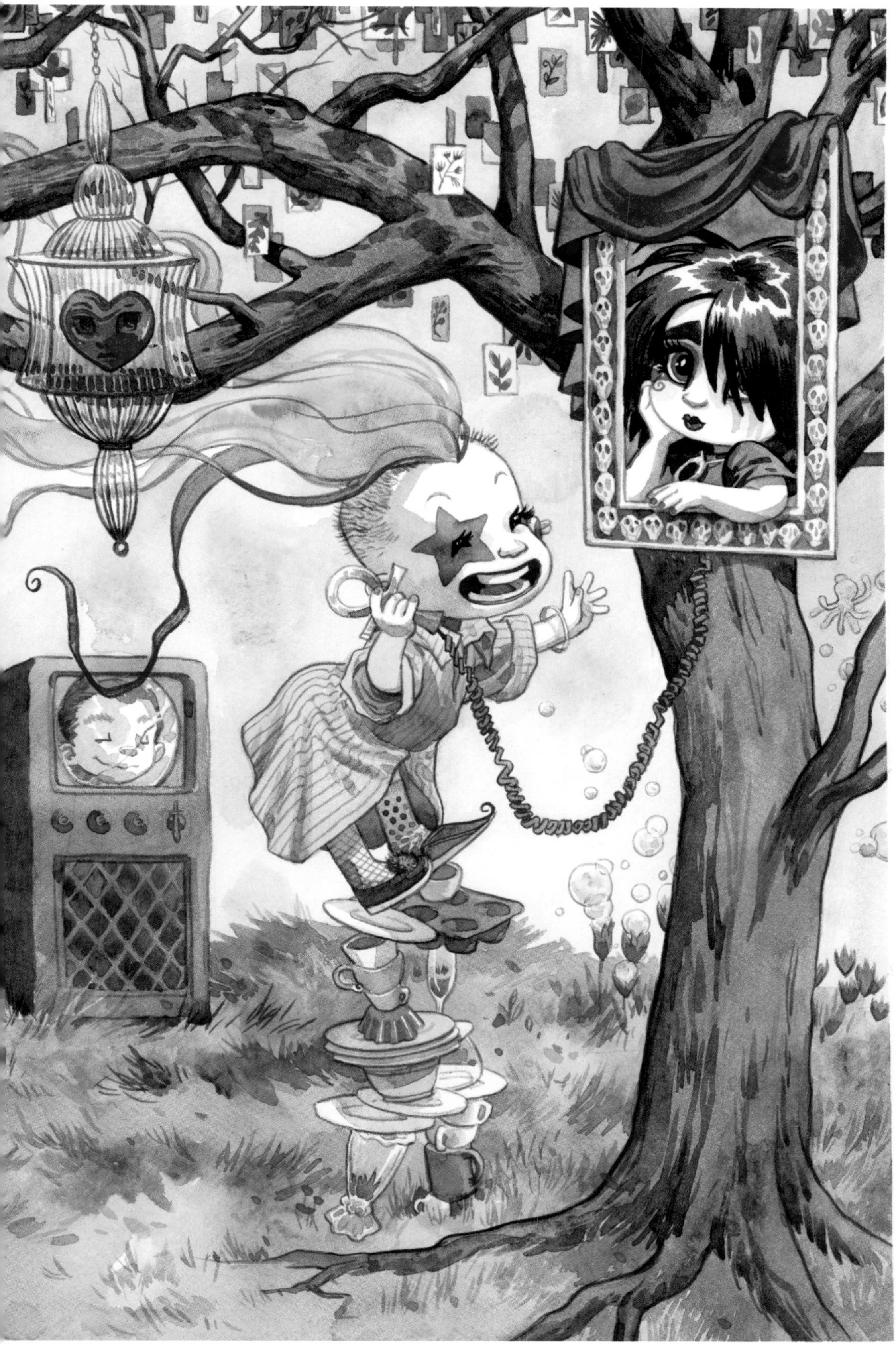

And she called Despair, in the misty place,
where the mirrors reflected nothingness
and the landscape tasted like sharp metal and tears.

The Princess Delirium chattered away, talking to each sibling about
the never empty pockets and the winged monkeys and the green faerie..
until she became tired and decided to go to bed.
"I must go to bed!" she said as she yawned.

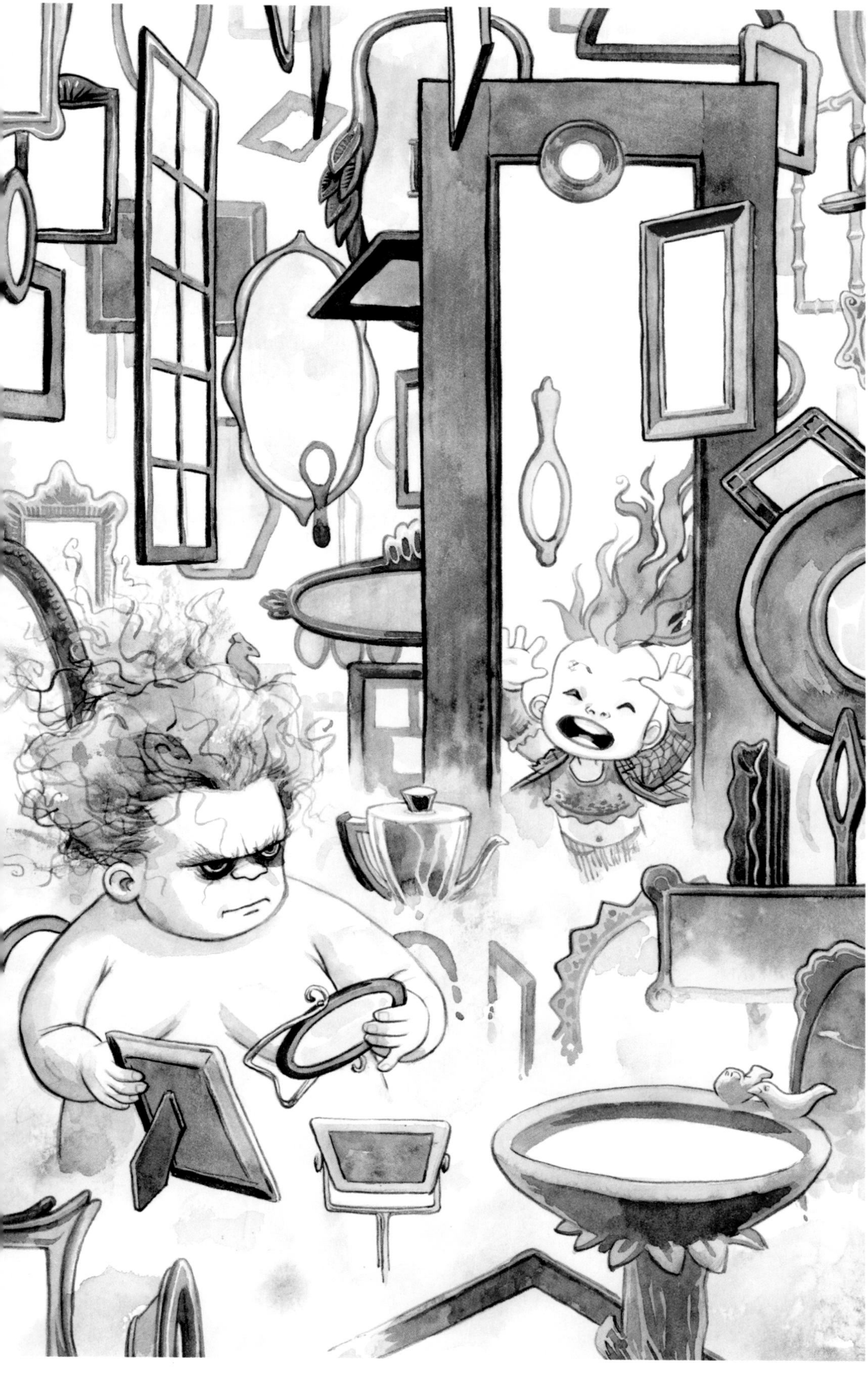

$\mathcal{B}$arnabas settled in next to her
and was just about to catch that rabbit when—
"OH, MY GRACIOUS ME!" cried the tinsel Princess.
"I have never seen my sister Despair smile! NEVER NO EVER!"

"Can't we talk about that in the morning?
whimpered Barnabas from under the covers.
After some shut-eye and nummy biscuits and a good long walk?"

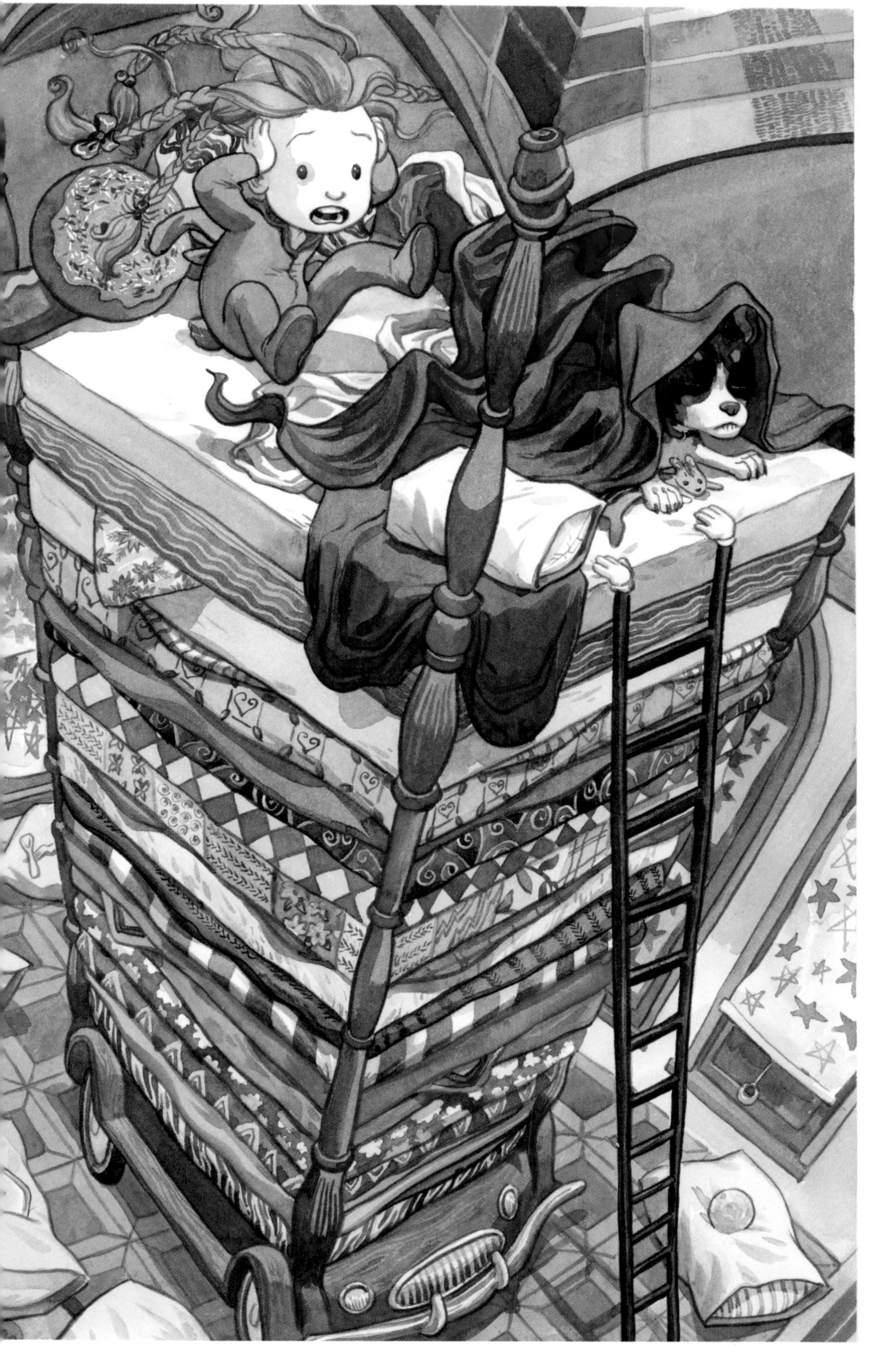

"Pretend I'm your sister — just for practice, look, see? I'm smiling —
and then you can start on her in the morning...
but now — bedways is bestways, right?" cried the pooped-out pup.

"Of course not, silly! There is nothing more important than
seeing someone smile! And it is SUPER SPECIALEST MOST GRANDIVEI
important when that someone is your very own sister!
Who you love lots and lots! With sugar on it! Right, silly doggie?"

"Right..." sighed Barnabas.

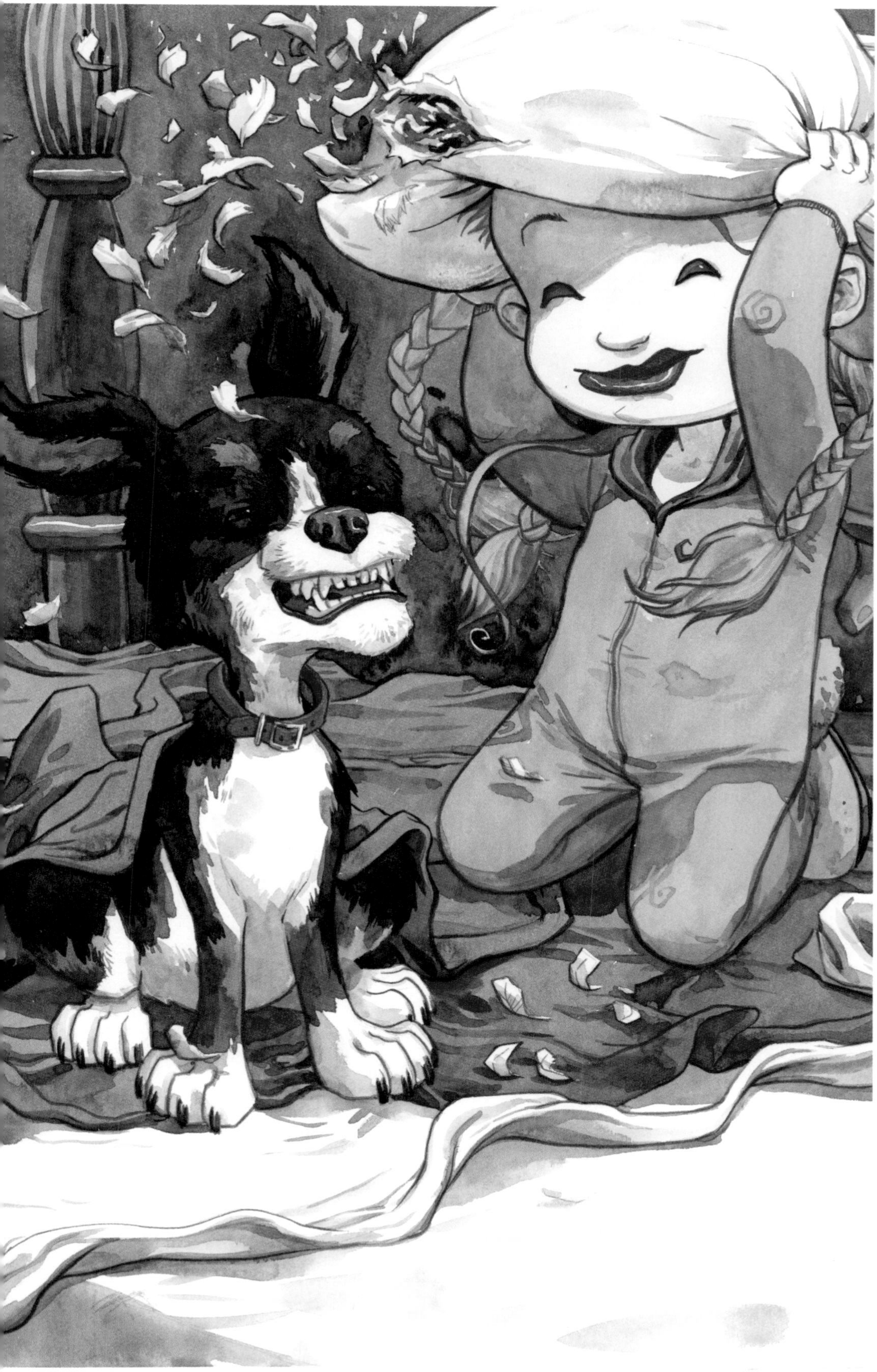

So Delirium put on her thinking cap for inspiration.
And she Thinked
Thunked and
Thoughtededed...
Until —

"Aha!" she exclaimed.

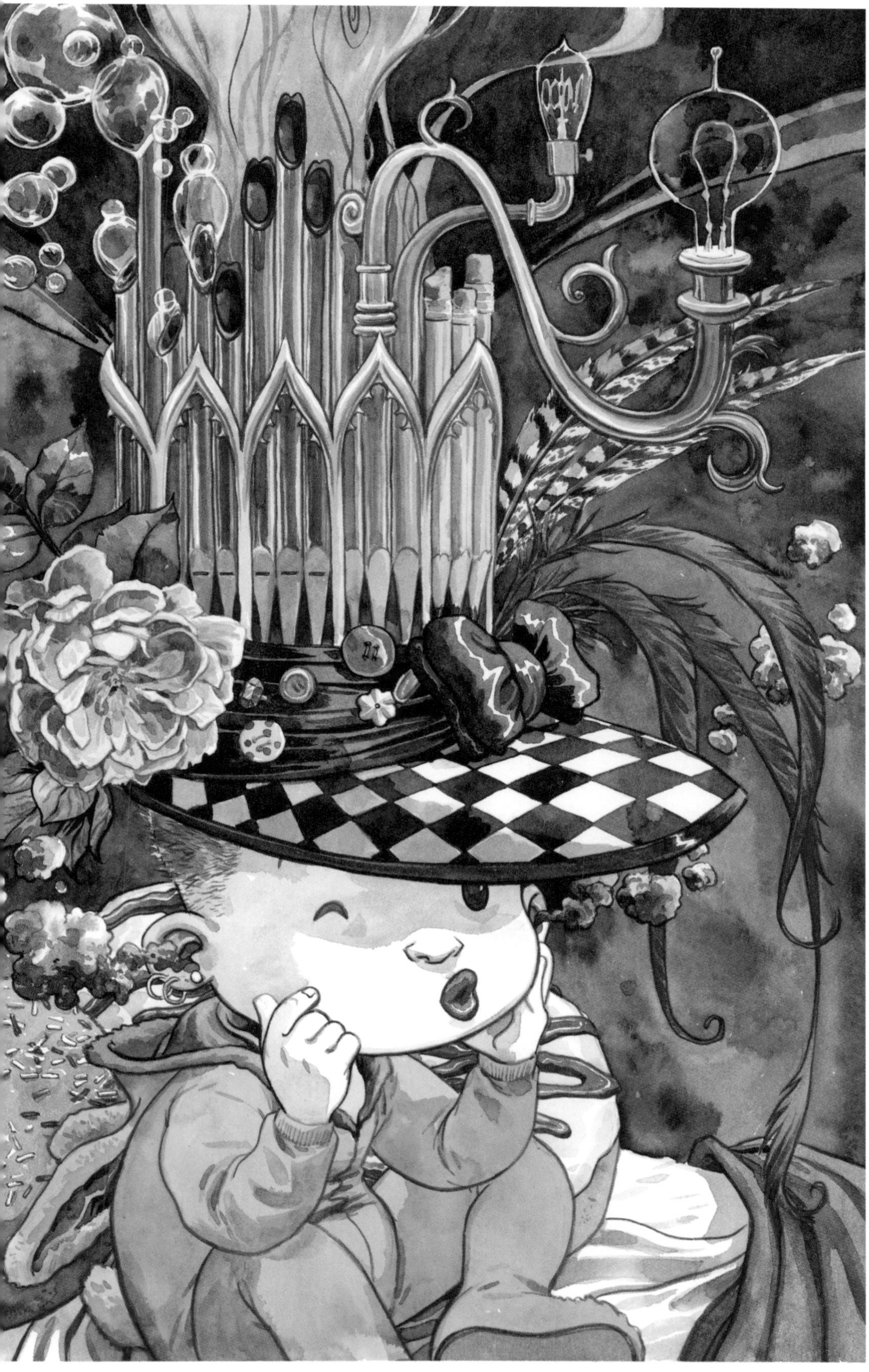

"Barnabas!" she said as she shook the puppy.
"You feel very velvety, my poochiepie!
But anyways — WHAT IS IT THAT EVERYONE LOVES MORE
THAN ANYTHING? MORE THAN ZUCCHINI TOAST AND
GLOCKENSPIELS AND THE TINY, SCARY, TOOTHITY FISH
THAT LIVE IN THE INKY PARTS OF THE OCEANS?"

"A nap?" replied Barnabas hopefully.

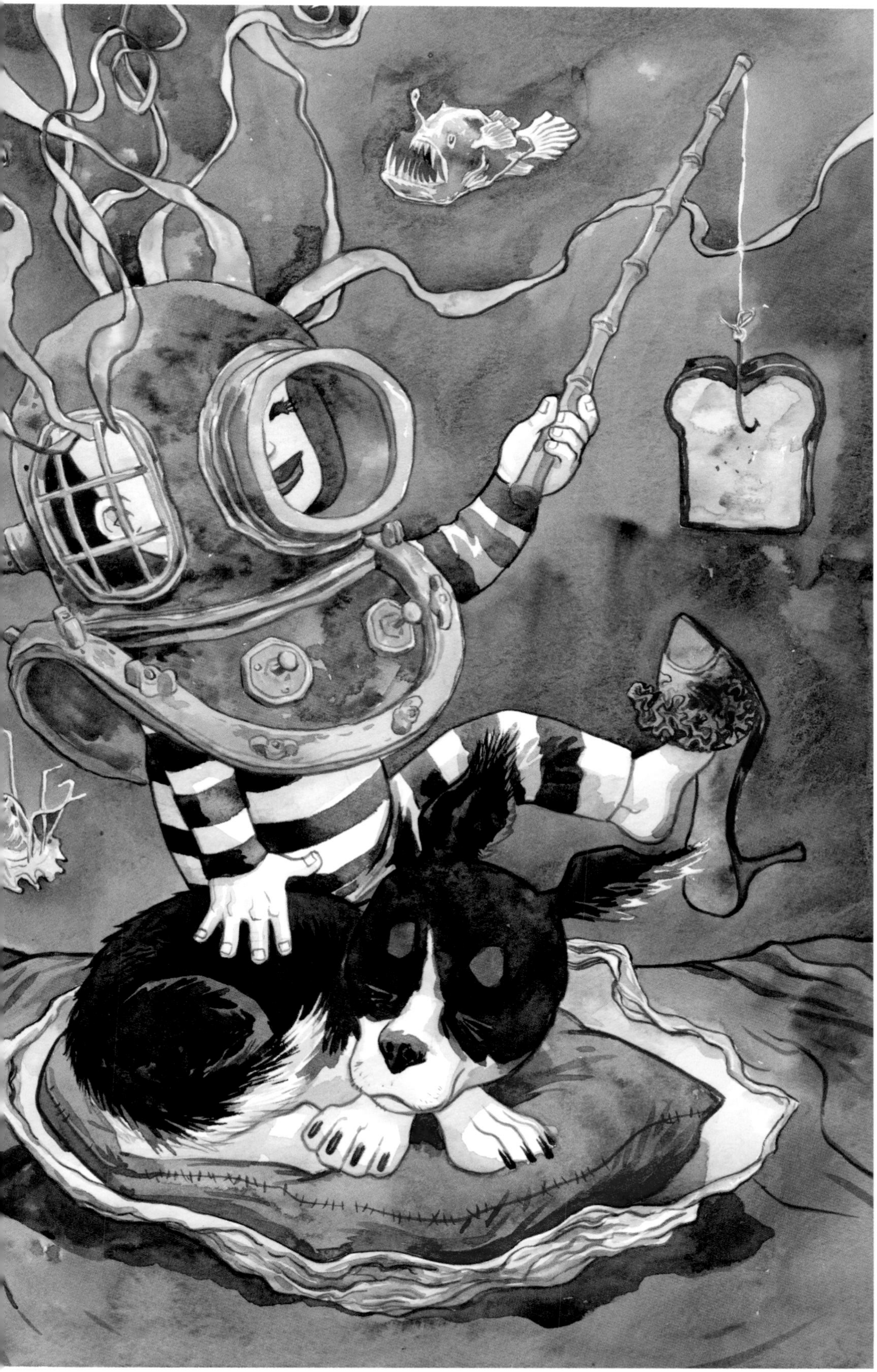

"NOooo!" giggled Delirium. "Guess again!"
"Table scraps?"
"NO! Again!"
"A game of fetch?"
"NO! Again again!"
"A squeaky toy?"
"Againagainagain!"
"A scratch on the belly, tug o' war, chasing a rabbit,
rolling around in something smelly, chewing an old shoe,
howling at the moon, barking at the mailman,
going to dog beach, sleepin' in front of a warm fireplace,
digging up the flowerbeds..." Barnabas stopped.

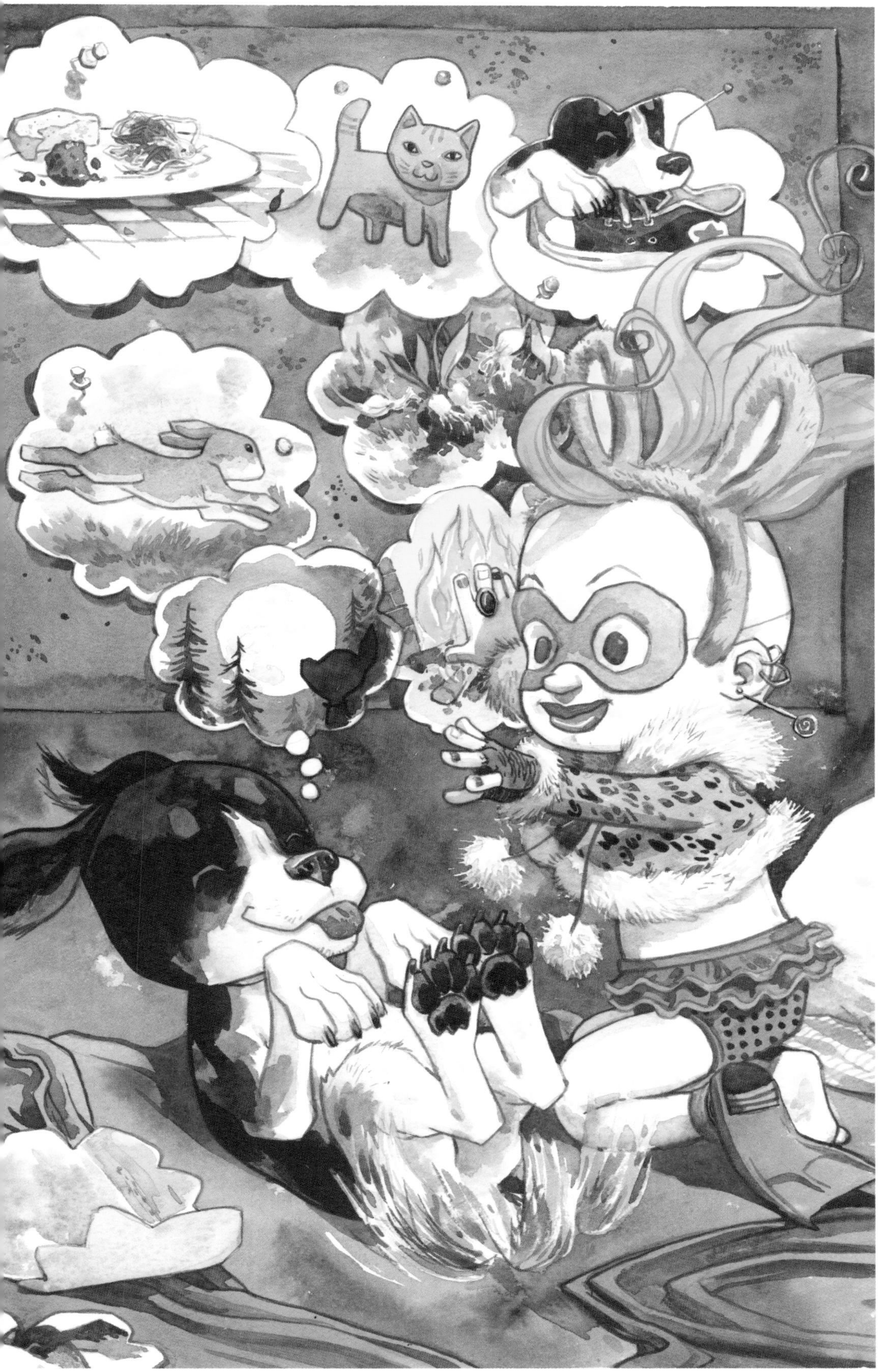

"How am I doing?" he asked.

"You are very funny, puppity dog!"

"But am I getting close?"

"Close to what?"

"The thing! The thing you asked me to guess!
The 'What is it that everybody loves' thing!"

"You mean a Party?" asked Delirium.

"...I suppose." said Barnabas. "I mean,
YOU were the one who asked the question in the first place!"

"Well then, I am correct!" exclaimed Delirium.

"So, what does that mean for us?"

"We are going to throw my sister, Despair, a party.
A surprise party! With sparkle and shine, sparkle and shine!"

"Come ON! We have so much to do!"

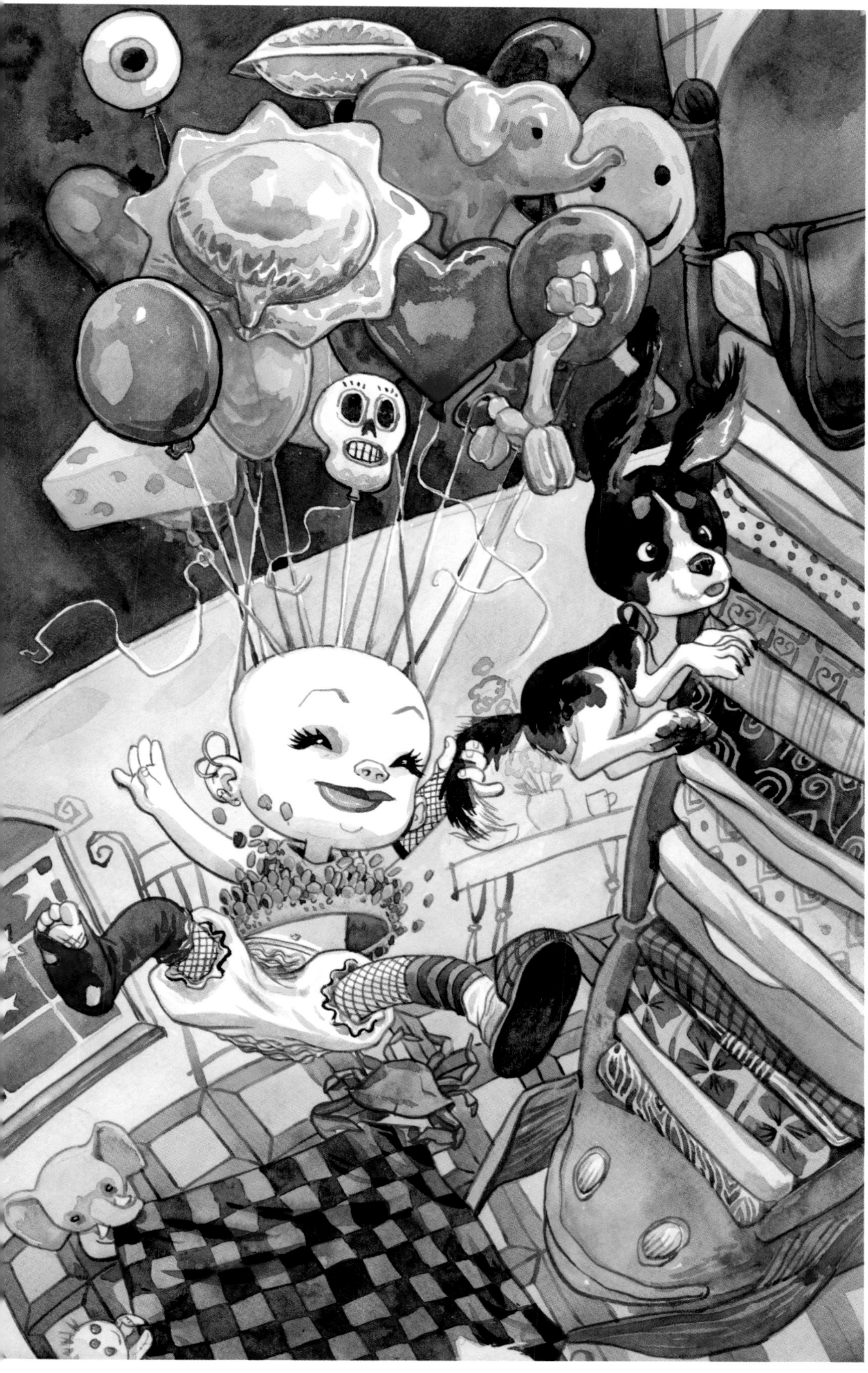

Delirium planned the party,
Barnabas made the invitations.
The realm was a Technicolor explosion of decoration.
A cake was created. A table was set.
Things that played music began to sing.
A door was knocked upon because some of the guests had arrived.

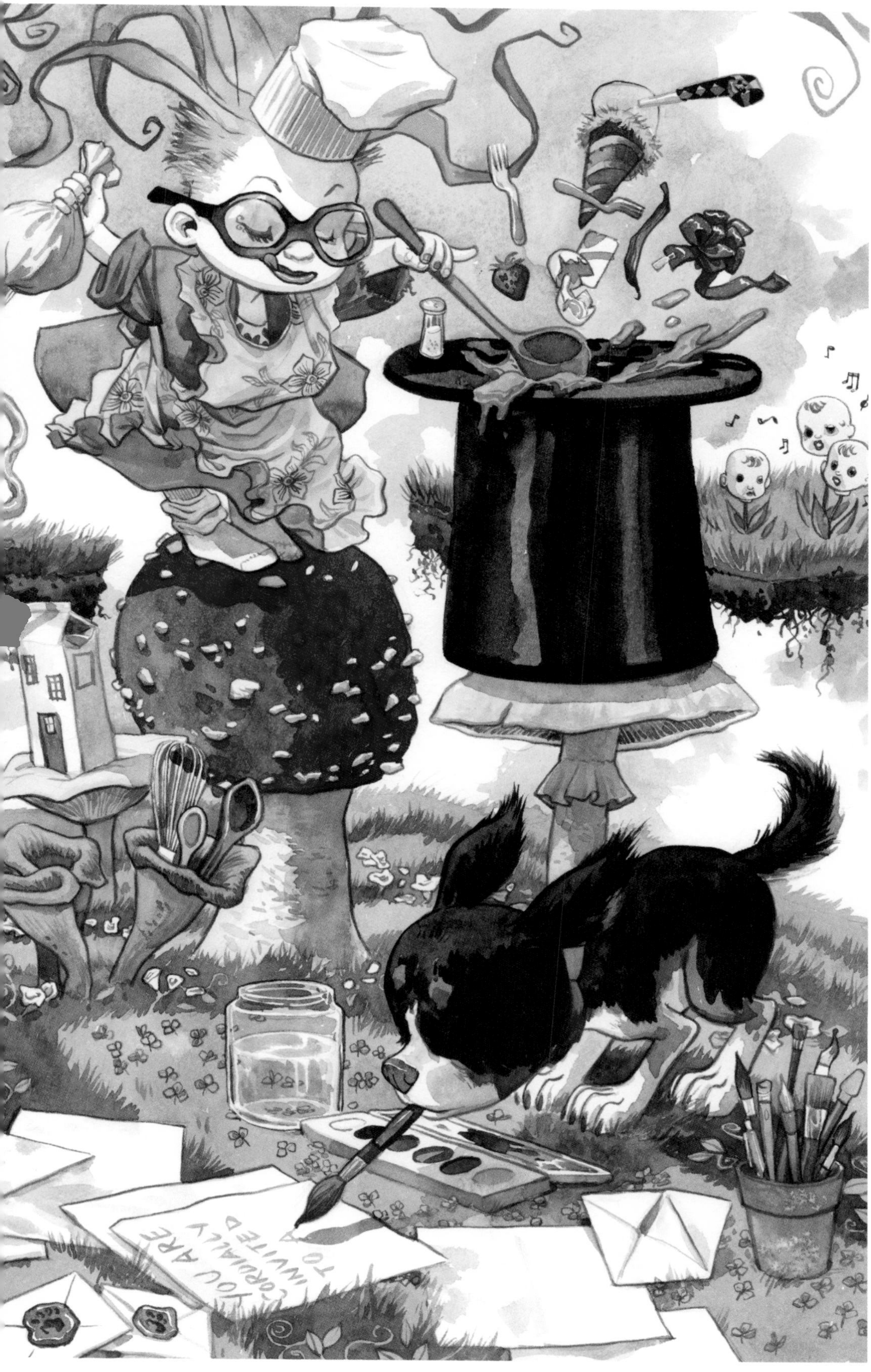
YOU ARE
CORDIALLY
INVITED
TO

"Oh! Where are your costumes?"
cried Delirium. "It's a fancy-dress party!"
"..." said the Family.
"Kiddo," said Barnabas.
"I'd call those getups 'costumes' any day of the week!"

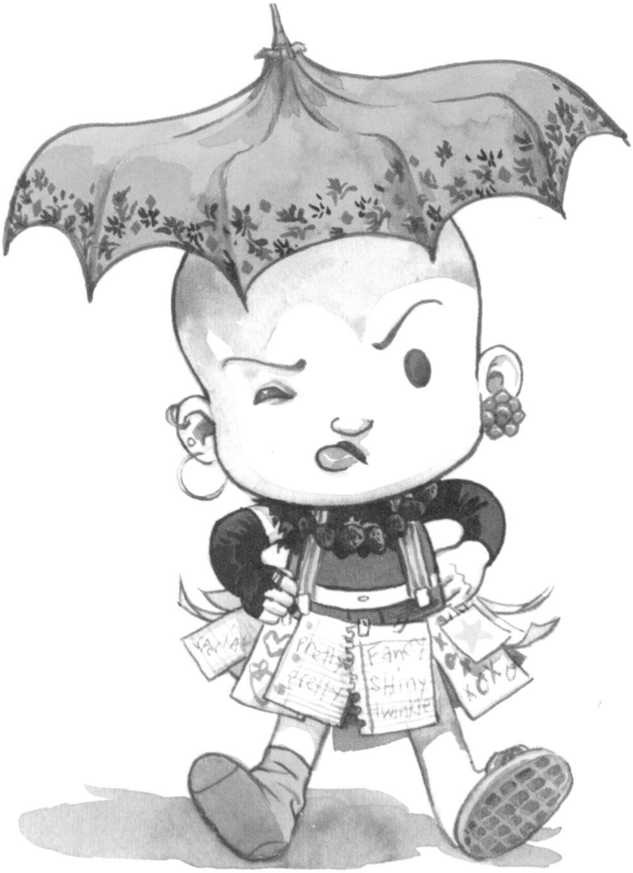
Pretty pretty
Fancy Shiny Twinkle
XOXO

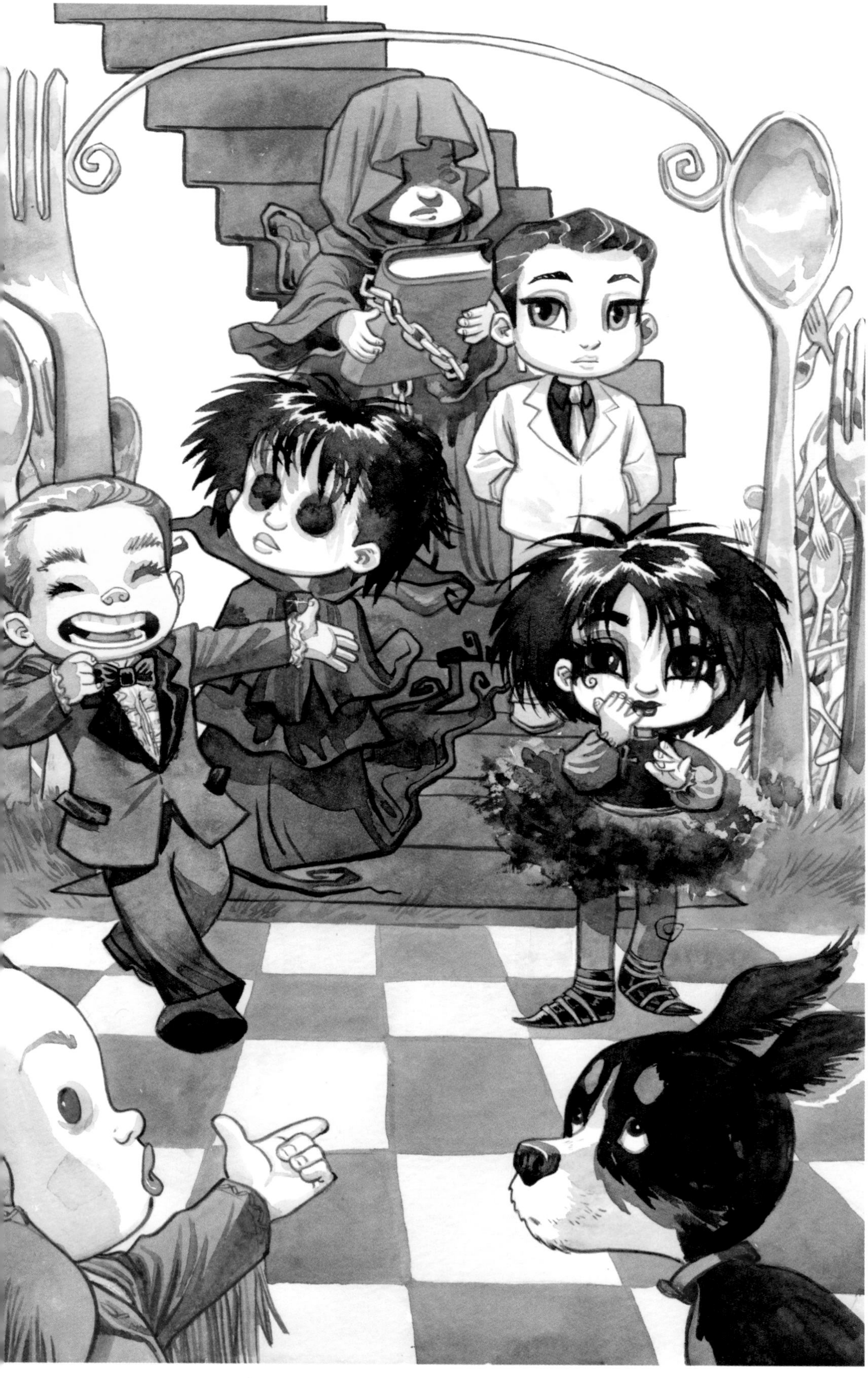

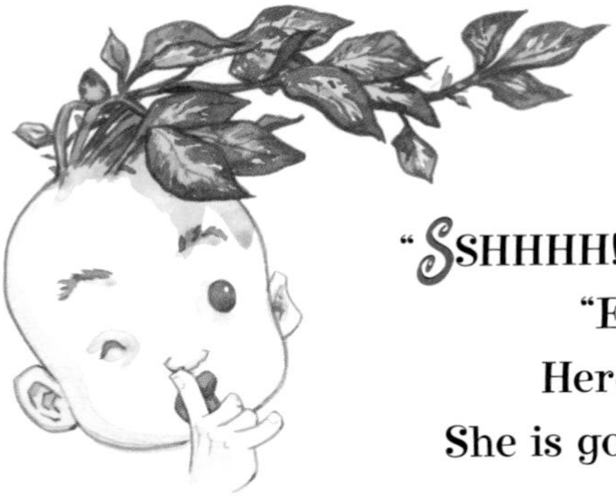

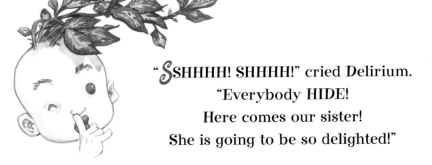

"SSHHHH! SHHHH!" cried Delirium.
"Everybody HIDE!
Here comes our sister!
She is going to be so delighted!"

Delirium created things for the family to hide behind.
The Door opened.
"SUUHH-PRIIIZE!!" Delirium shouted as
the family burst out to greet their sister.

". . ." said Despair, her face set as if in stone.
"SURPRISE! SURPRISE! SURPRISE! SURPRISE!"
giggled Delirium as she danced about the room.
Yet, Despair only said, ". . ."
And did not smile.

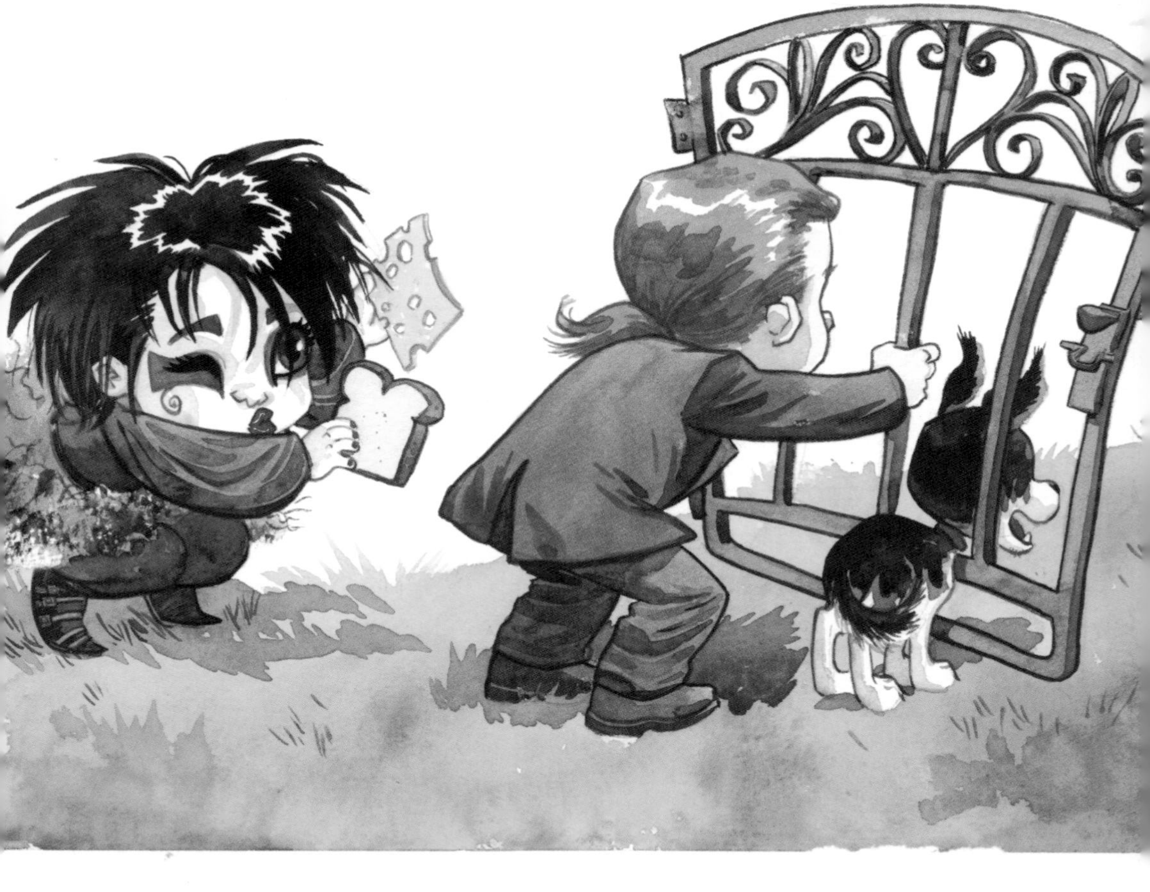

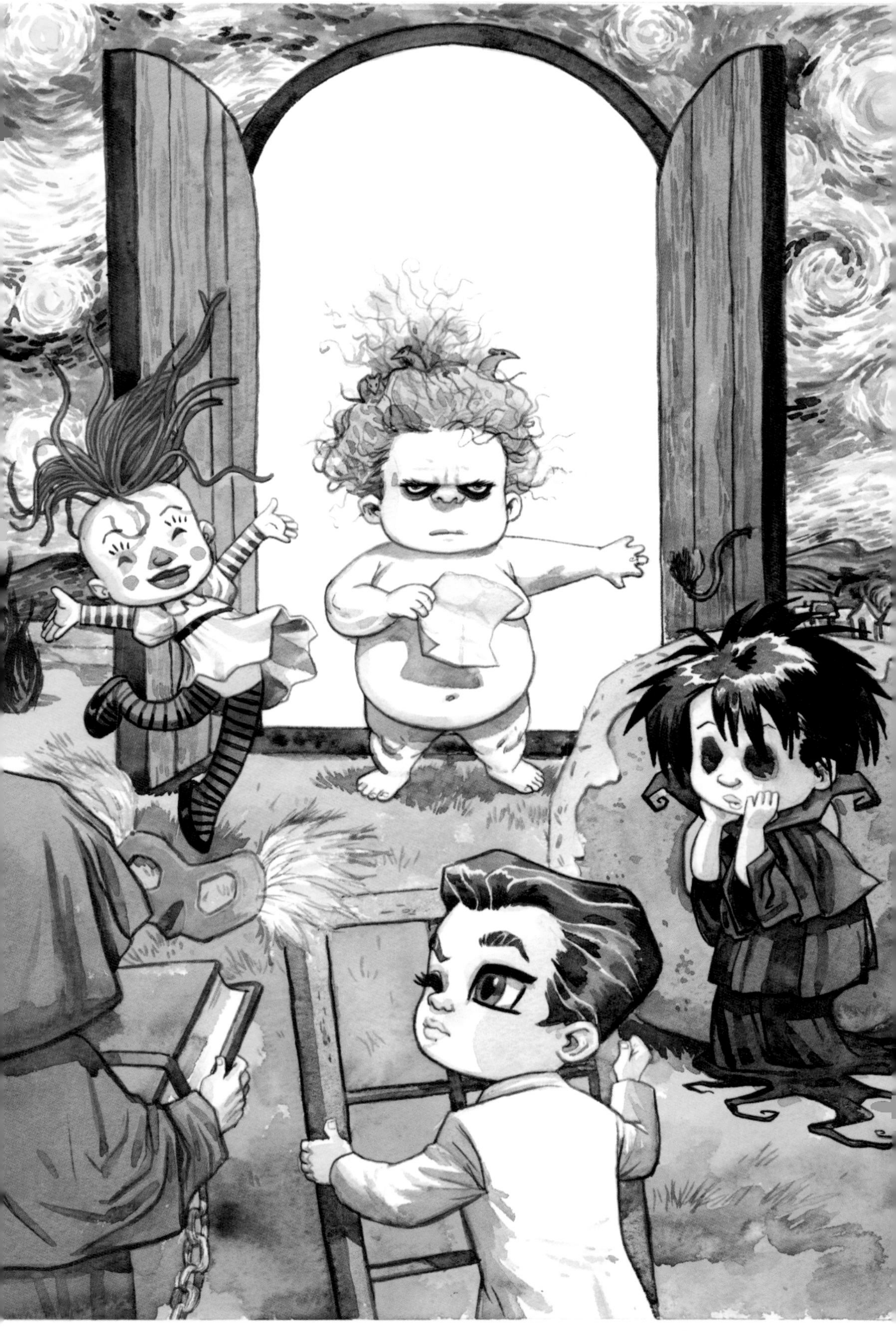

Not one to be discouraged, little Delirium pirouetted about.

"Look, sister Despair! Look!" cried Delirium as she pointed to the decorations that hung from the edges of the sky, "See the twinkles and the brights, and the sparkles and the floofs? I made them all by myself! For only you! It took LOTS of concentration, but I did so make them all by my lonesome!! Well, perhaps Barnabas helped a little bit with some of the more complicated parts. But still... "TaaDaaa!" Despair glanced around yet only said ". . ."

And still she did not smile.

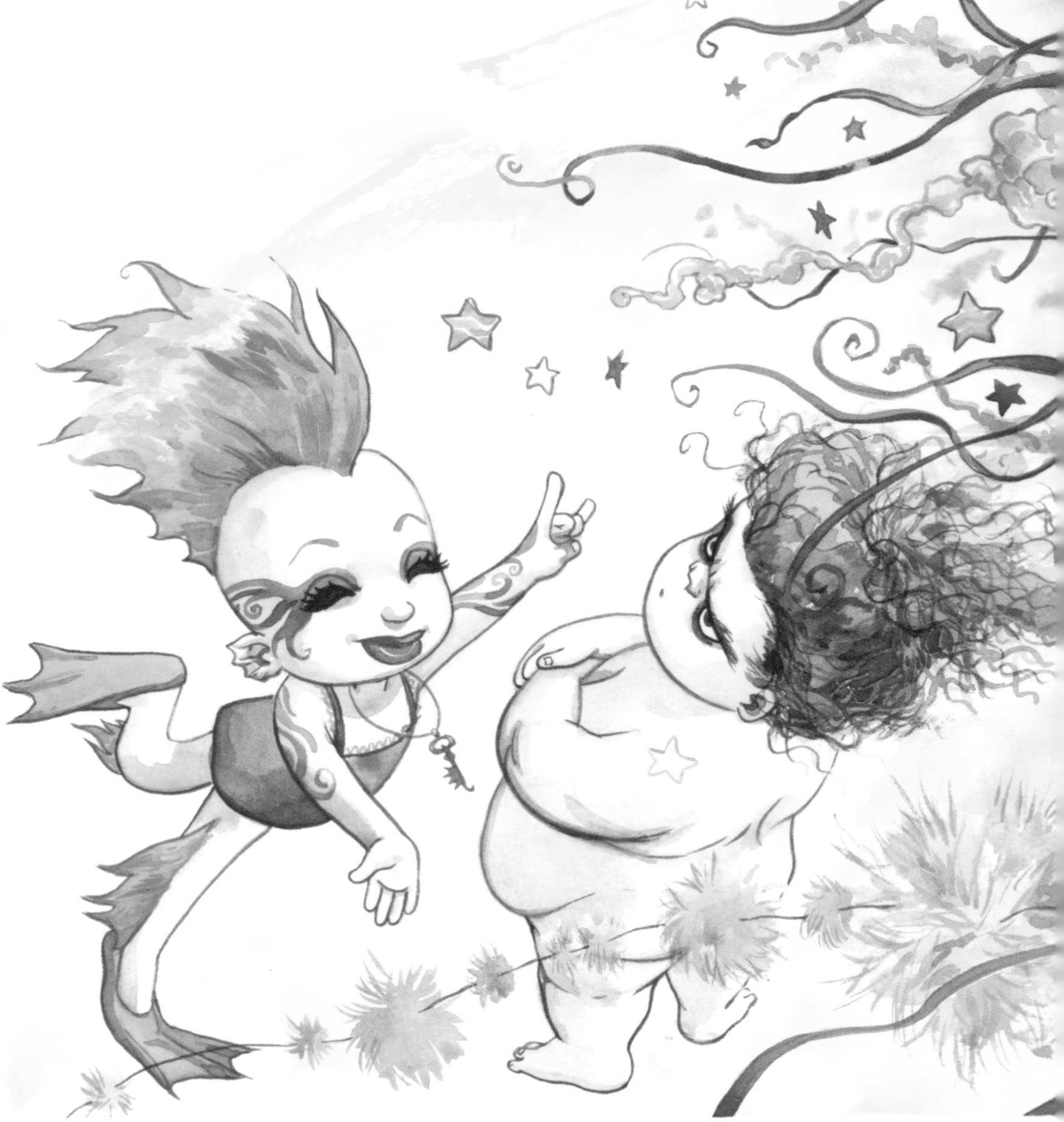

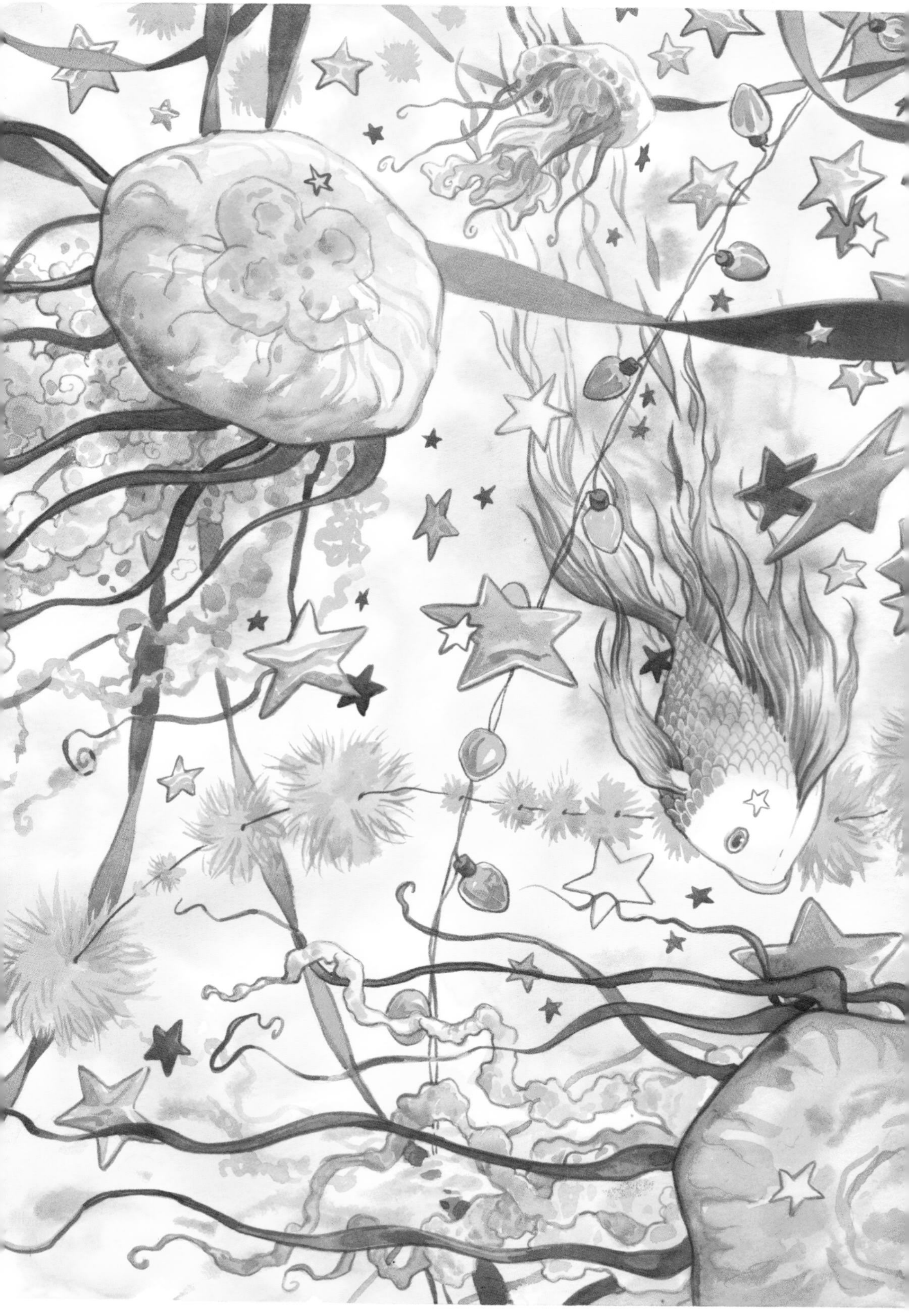

$\mathcal{B}$arnabas whispered to Dream, Delirium's older brother.
"Maybe...she doesn't understand the Surprise party is for HER!"

"Do you not feel sudden wonder or amazement because
of this unexpected gathering of your siblings?" asked Dream.
"..." said Despair.
Still, Delirium refused to be dispirited.

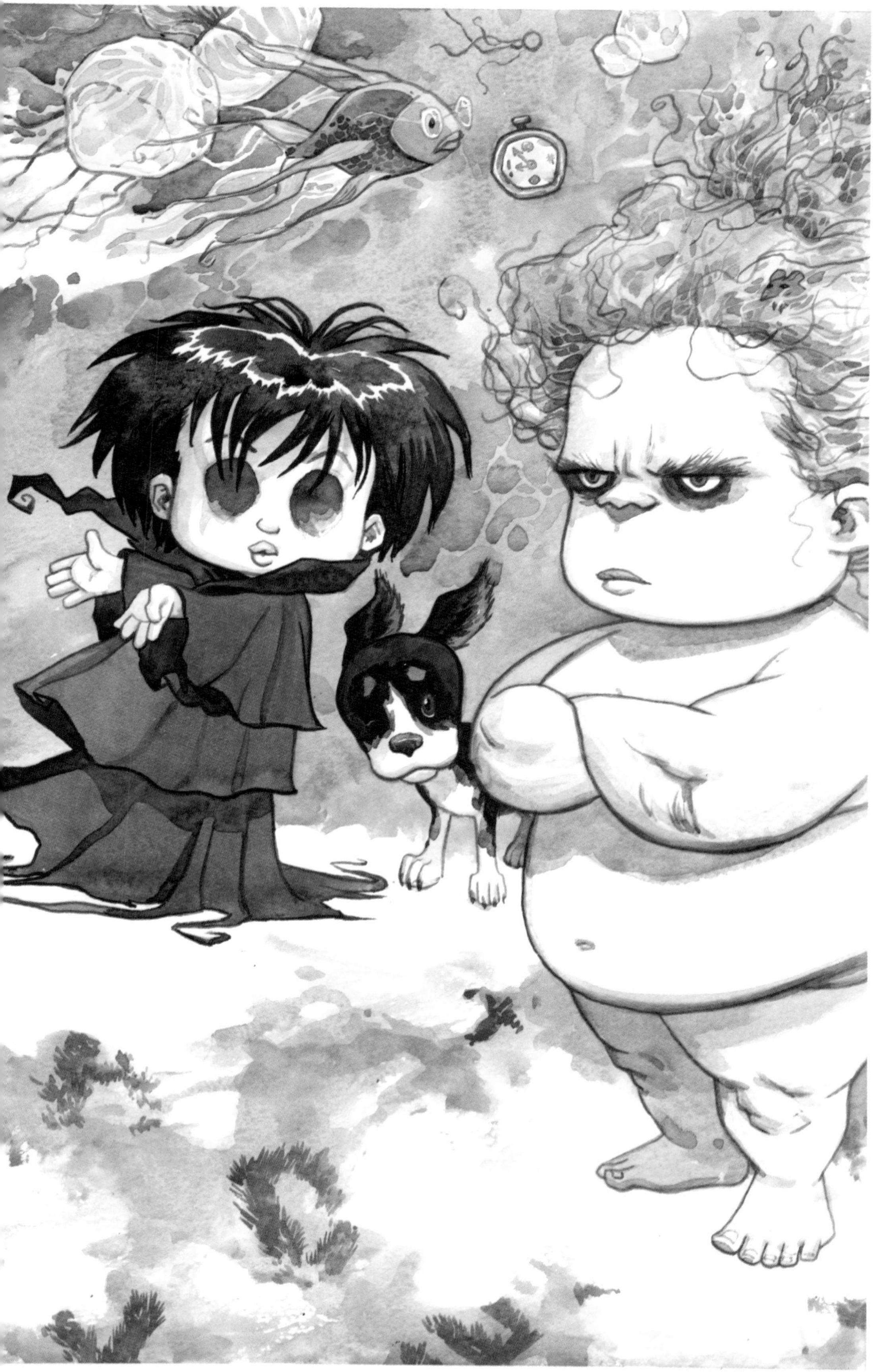

"Oh Ho!" cried Delirium.
"I know what you're waiting for!"
Delirium called to her puppy. "Barnabas! Fetch!"
Barnabas dashed off and rustled around behind a curtain.
He tugged and tugged at the velvet cloth until...

"SUHHH-PRIEEEZZE!" shouted Delirium as she smiled
and pointed to a towering confection.
"..." was the only response from a sour-faced Despair.

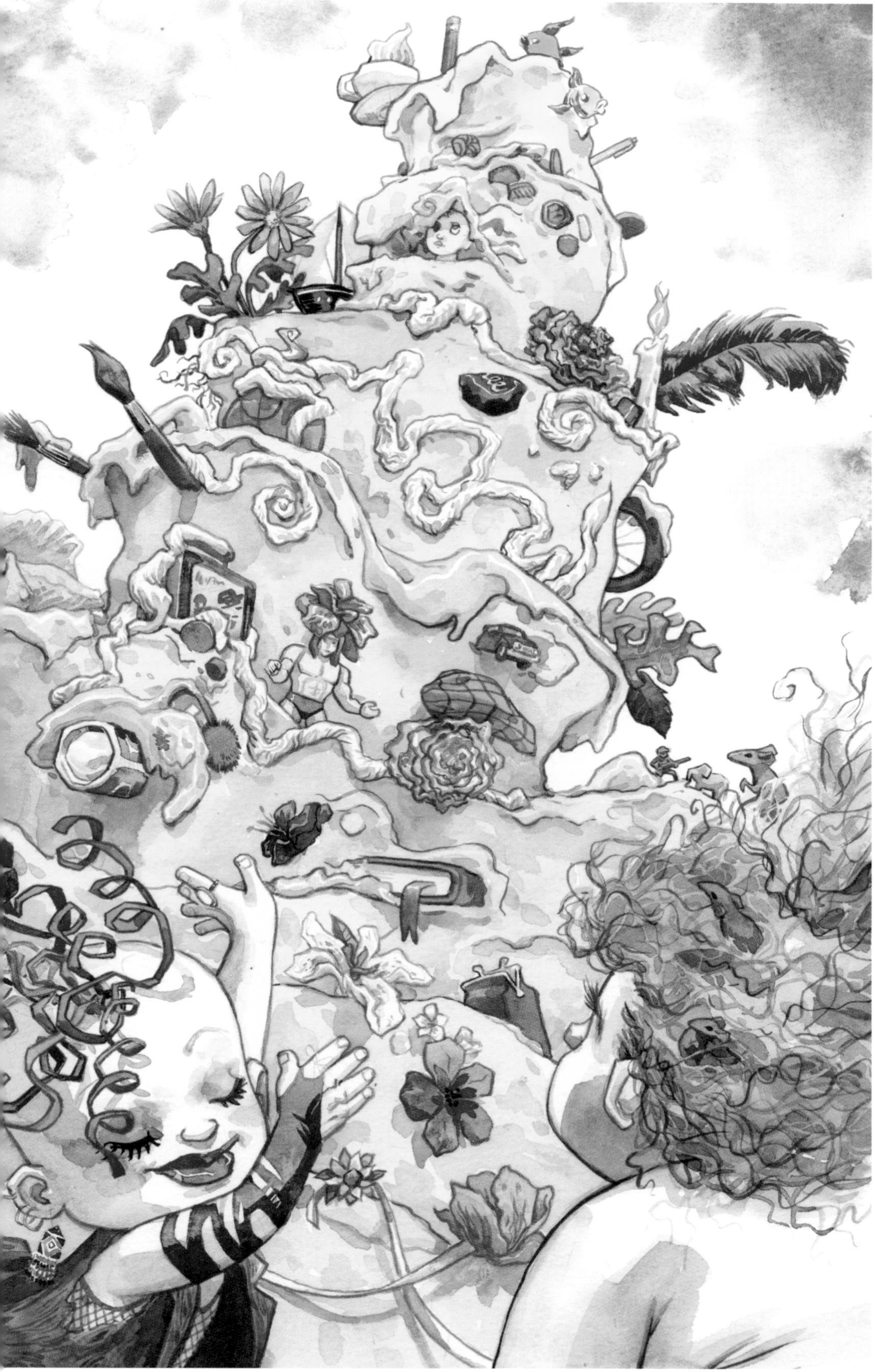

$\mathcal{E}$ach family member was given a piece of "cake."

"See, Barnabas! I told you everyone would like a surprise cake!
It has all the things everyone likes!"

The family politely smiled and courteously nibbled
at the unusual treats that were set before them.
However, Despair sat, unmoved and said, "..."

"Do you not appreciate the effort required of our sister in
concocting this semblance of pastry for your enjoyment?" asked Dream
"..." replied Despair.

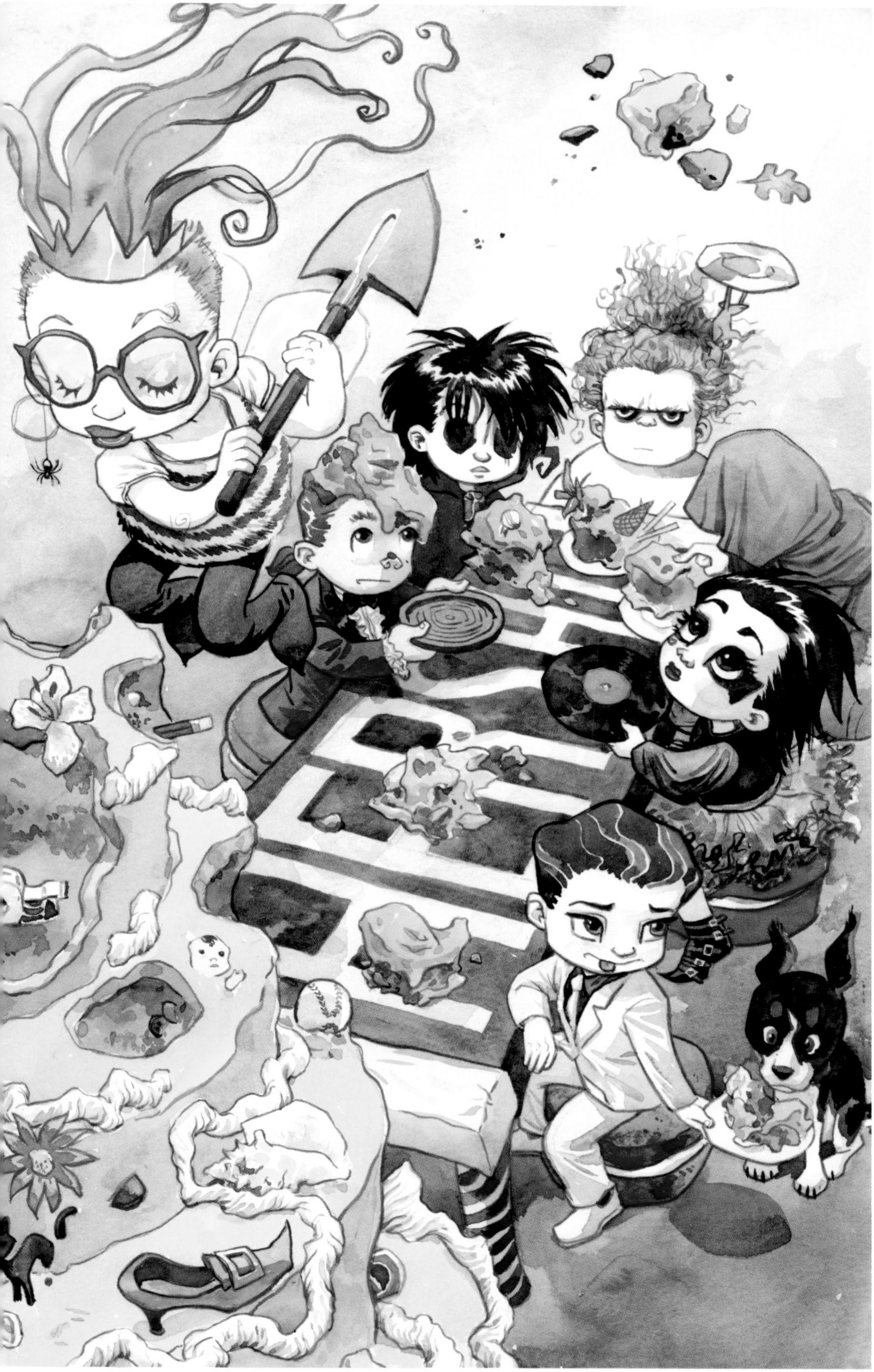

Not to be deterred, Delirium jumped up and squealed.

"OH, I know what you are waiting for, I do!"

Delirium pushed her sister down into a comfy chair
and placed a crown of sorts upon her tousled hair.
"Today you get to wear the Princess Hat for it is your special day!"
"Now close your eyes!" insisted Delirium as she helped her sister
by covering Despair's eyes with her own little fingers.

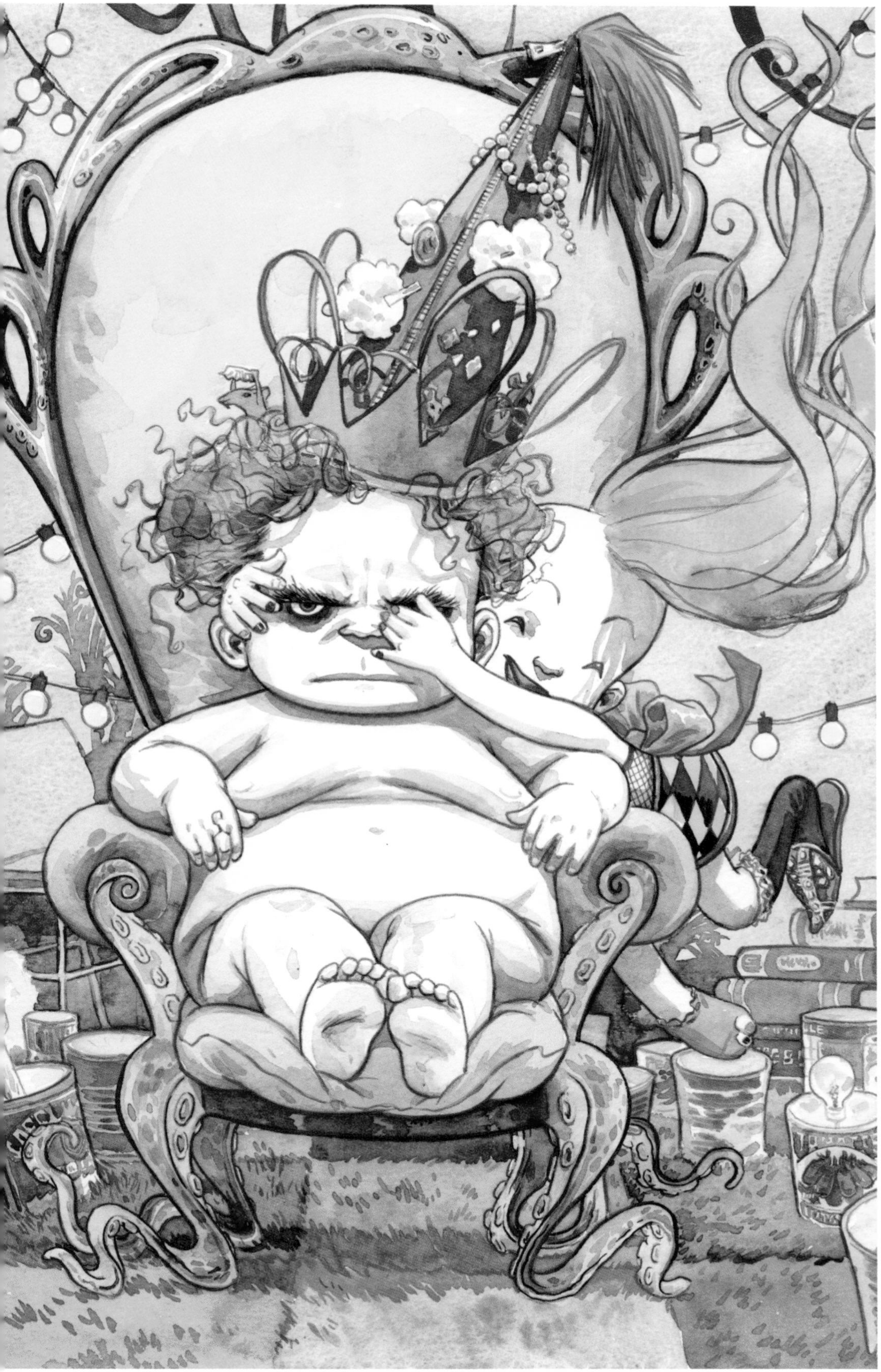

"SOOOO-PRYYYYYYZE!!" Delirium shouted.
The Family was gathered before Despair
with colorful packages tied with extravagant bows.
"It is PRESENTS! PREZZIES! GIFTIES for YOU!"
cried Delirium. "Come on, everybody! Who shall go first?"

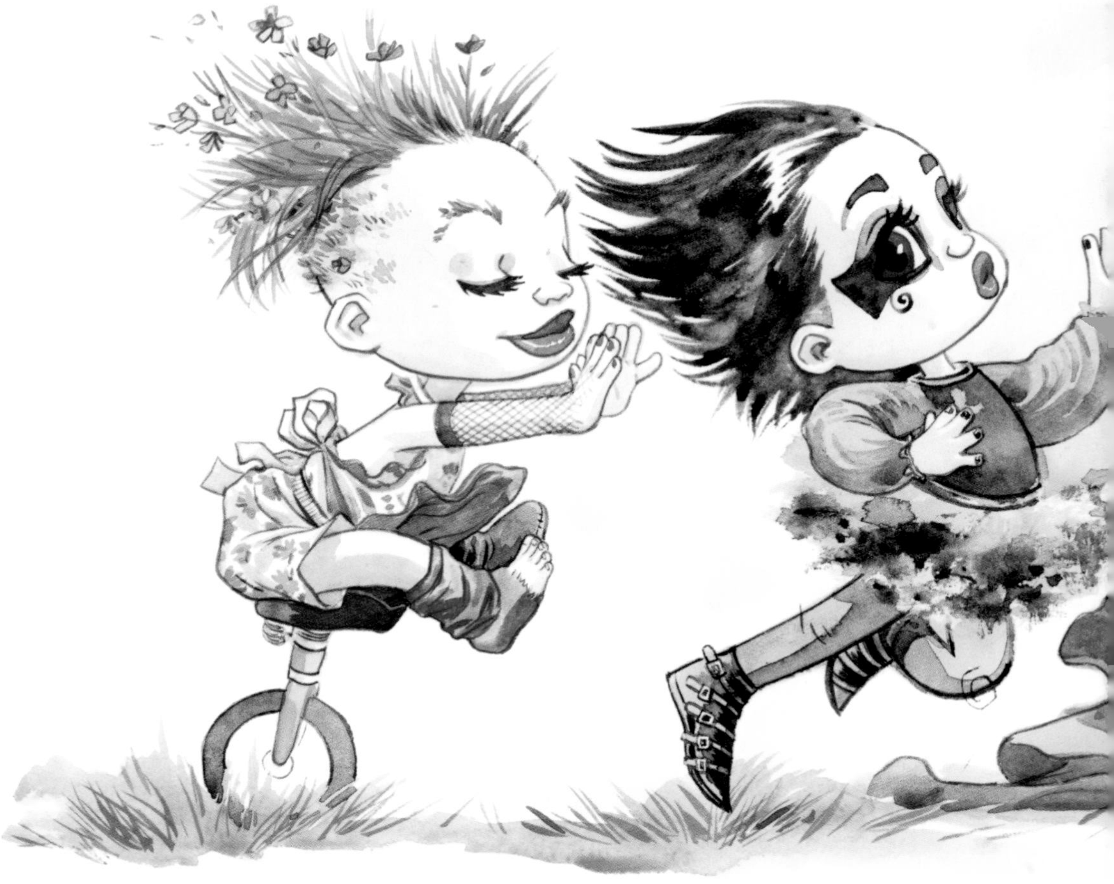

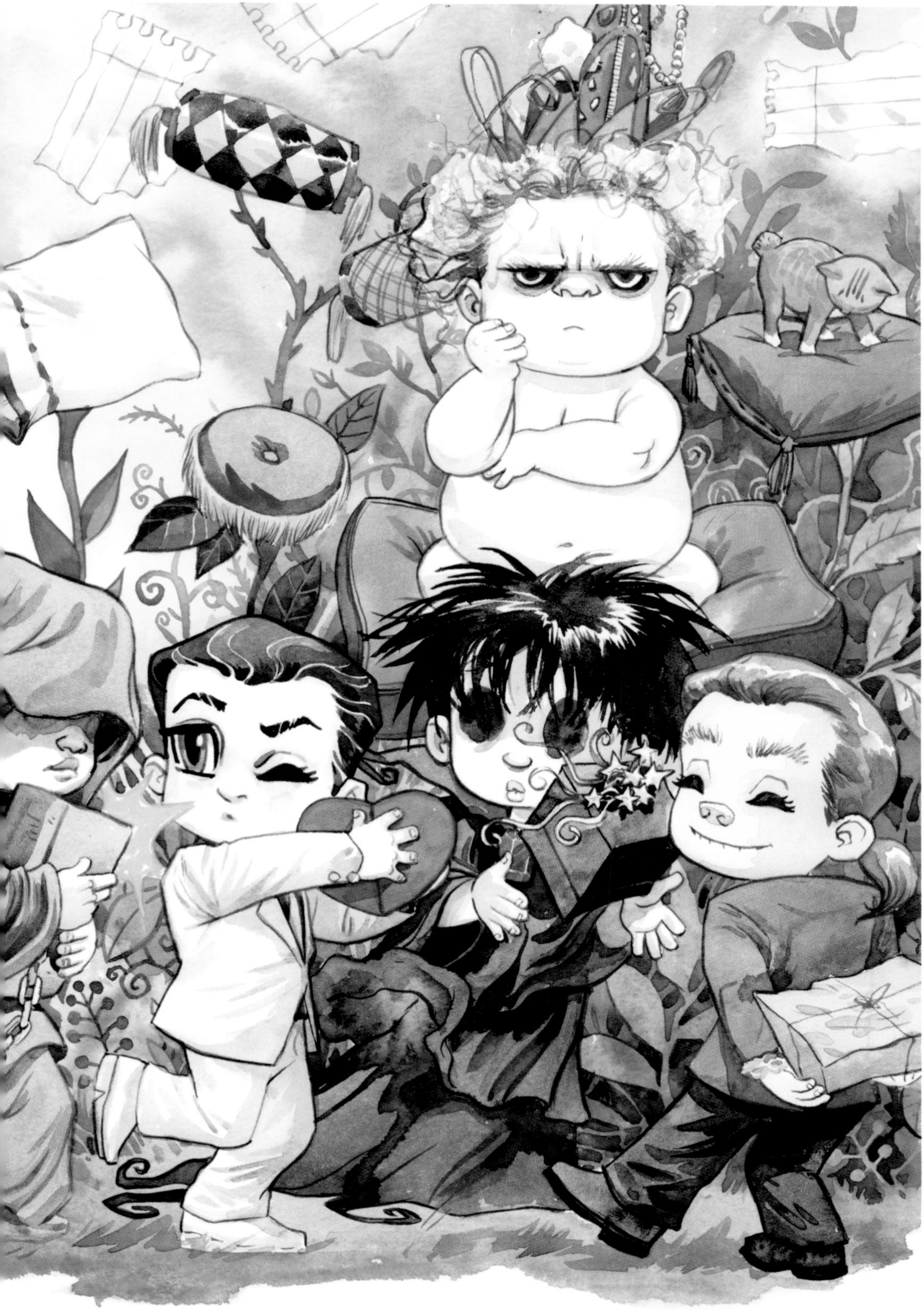

$\mathcal{D}$estiny stepped forward.
He held the Big Book in front of Despair.
In addition to a chain, it also sported a bow.

"Untie the ribbon, sister, and you shall see a page out of my book.
On it you shall see a pleasant, prosperous path in my garden.
You can walk it easily without difficult or painful choices."
"Wuf!" said Barnabas! "That is a good gift!"
Yet Despair simply stared and said, ". . ."
Destiny closed his book and drifted to the side.

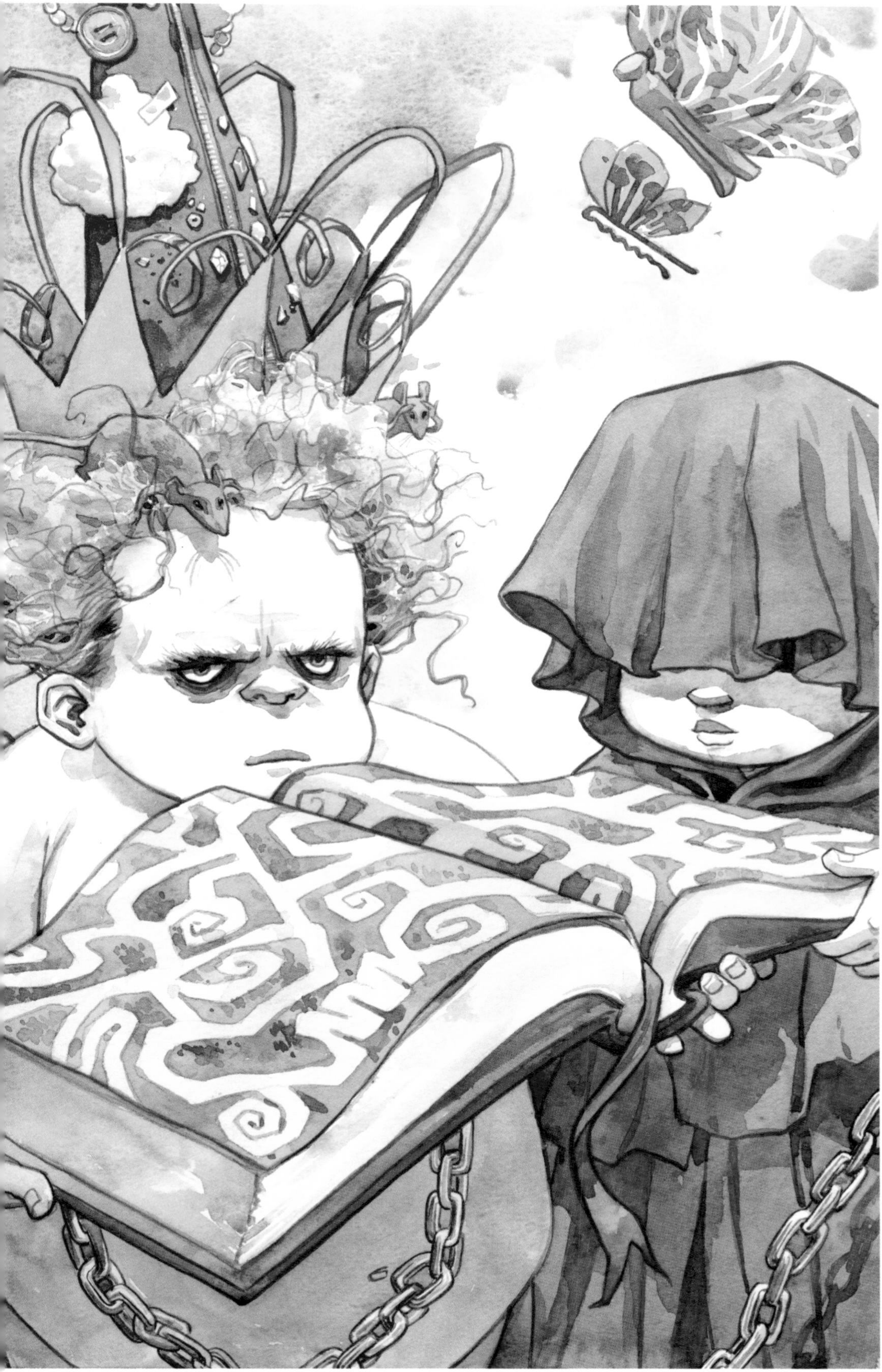

Next, Dream approached his sister.
In his hands he held a dark, velvet box with a bow of silver stars.

Despair opened the box to find a perfect crystal sphere.
"Embrace this while you rest, my sister,
and your slumber shall be filled with the most pleasant of imaginings...
your favorite tales forever saved within, and never
shall you be troubled by a nightmare."
"Woof! That is a good gift, too!"
Despair did not take the sphere but gazed into the box and said, ". . ."
Dream sighed a heavy sigh, closed the box, and moved to the side.

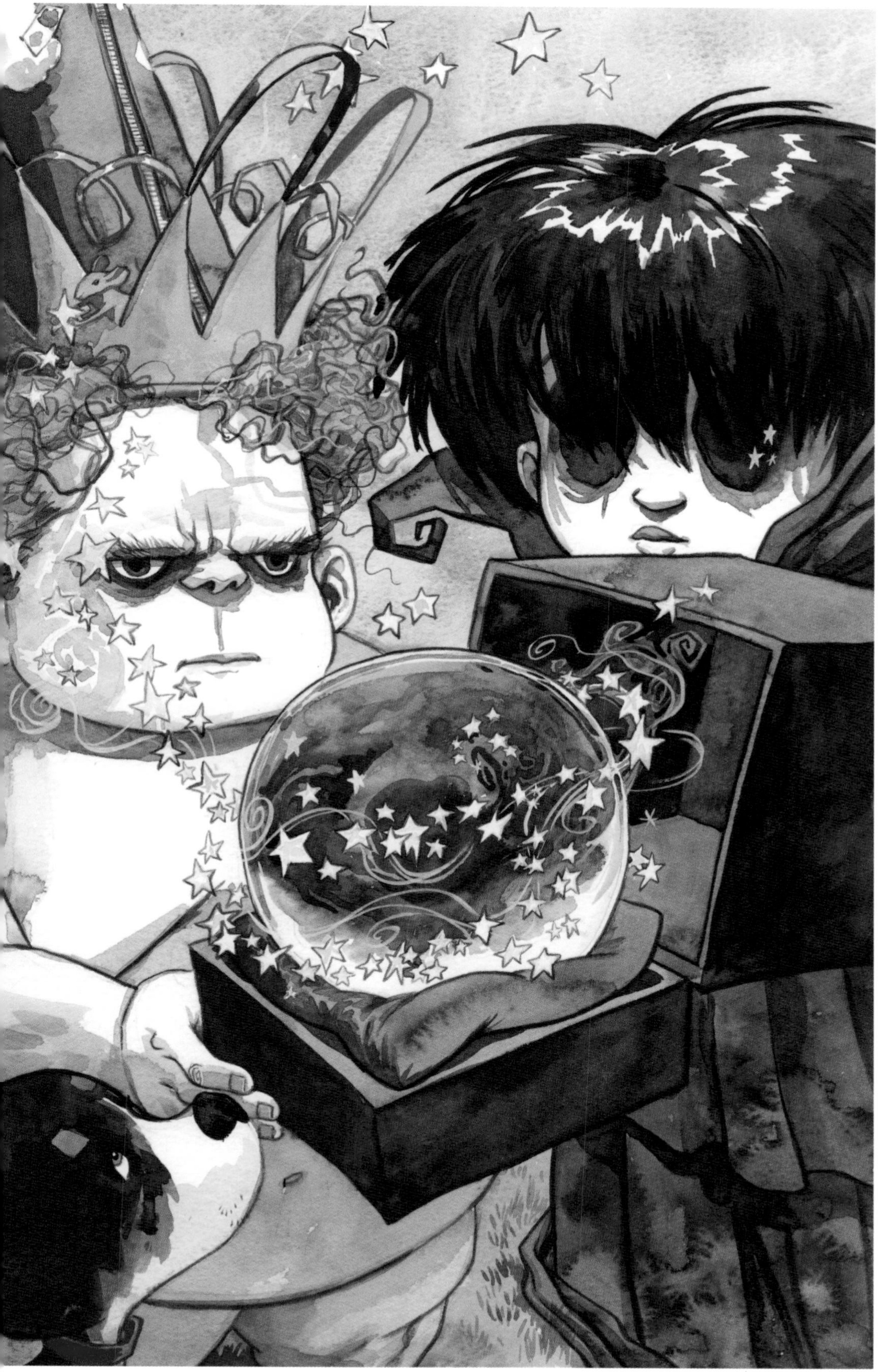

Desire leaned in close to its twin sister Despair.
In its hands it held a silken, heart-shaped box.

Desire pulled on the satiny ribbons, lifted the lid
to uncover a shiny, heart-shaped locket on a delicate silver chain.
"With this bauble around your neck, you shall be the object
of all hearts' longing. All that they need, all that they want
and all that they crave...you shall be muse and inspiration,
wish and want and longing..."
"Woof Woof!" said a very impressed Barnabas.
But Despair did not put the locket around her neck.
She sat and stared and said, ". . ."
Desire snapped the box shut, cast its gaze down and slid away.

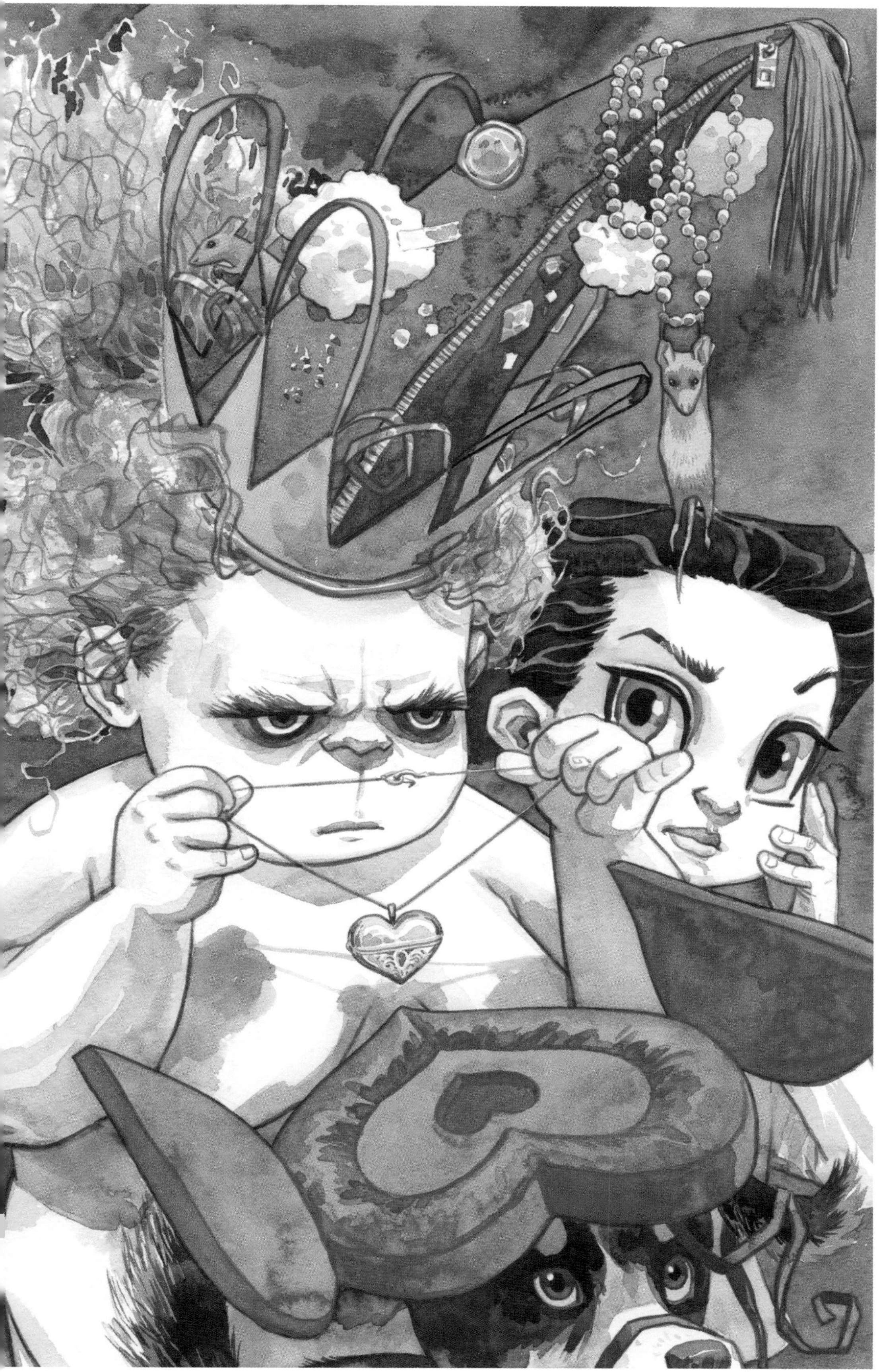

Destruction bounded toward his sister, a hastily wrapped box
in his hands. "Tear away at the wrapping!" he chortled.
"I can always make more!"

Despair used her fishhook-shaped sigil ring to cut through
the many layers of packing tape that held the flaps of the box shut.
Inside there was a china teacup filled with wet sand.

"In that cup is a universe of your own making, my sister!
You can shape mountains and buildings and rivers and valleys!
You can shape creatures and beings of your own design!
And, if you tire of them, you can smooth it flat and begin again!"
Destruction said proudly.
"Wooof!" snuffed Barnabas! "That is such a cool present!"
But Despair only said, ". . ."
Destruction was deflated and shuffled out of the way.

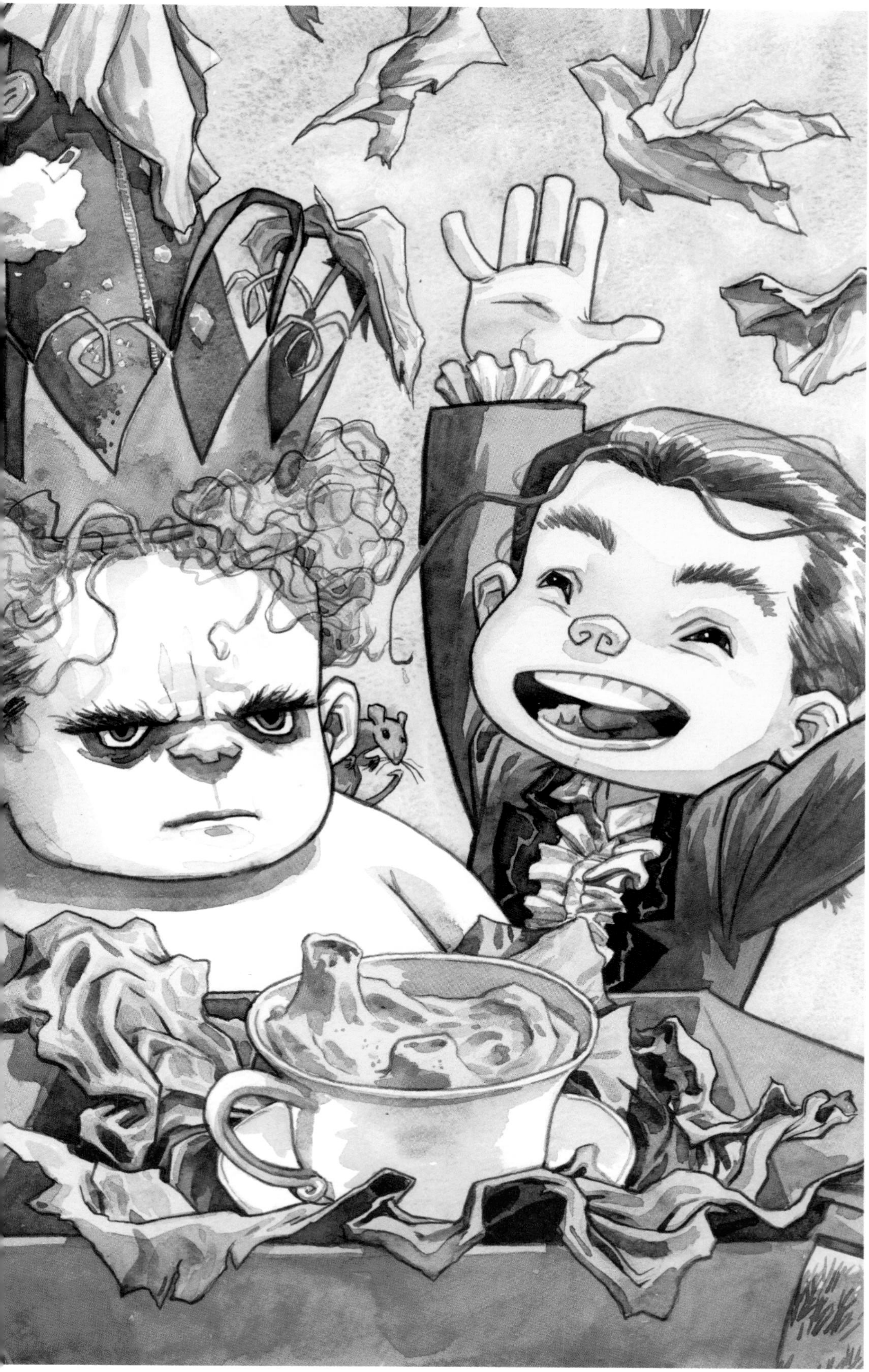

Next came the eldest sister, Death, who always smiled so sweetly.
She clasped her hands in front of her in the shape of a clamshell.
"Inside here is my gift for you, dear sister."

She opened her hands to reveal an empty space.

"When you require it of me, I shall come to you.
You will find eternal peace and calm.
All you have to do is take my outstretched hand."
Her serene demeanor and angelic face made the whole family smile...
And Barnabas said, "Ruff!"
Still, Despair only said, "..."
and did not smile.

Her eldest sister's rosebud mouth turned down in dismay
as she, too, moved to the side.

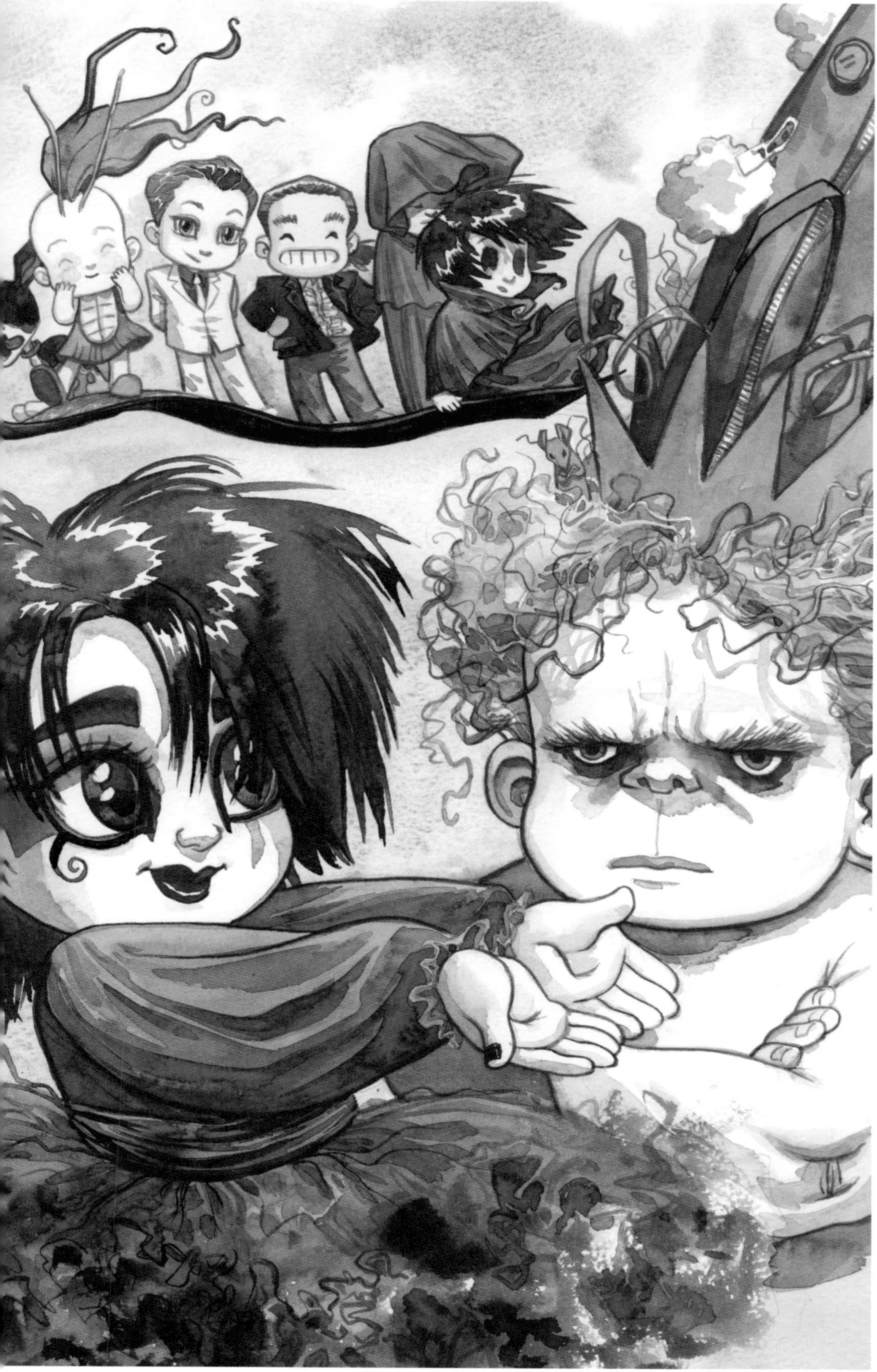

The sky turned grey. The brights turned dim.
The sparkles fizzled and the floofs flopped flumpily.
Delirium was despondent. Barnabas was fed up.
The rest of the Family was depressed.
Their hearts were filled with sadness.
Delirium's eyes filled with tears.
Her chin got all crinkly and her lip began to quiver.
"I failed, my doggie! I wanted to do my sister a happy,
but nothing was right!" wept Delirium. Barnabas whimpered.
Hearing her fragile sobs, the rest of the family began to cry as well.
Soon everyone was filled with hopelessness and gloom.

The fog of despondency hung thick around them.
And as Despair looked out on all of the
miserable faces, she made a bemused little snort.
Barnabas turned his head to the sound
and saw Despair's turned-up cheek and...

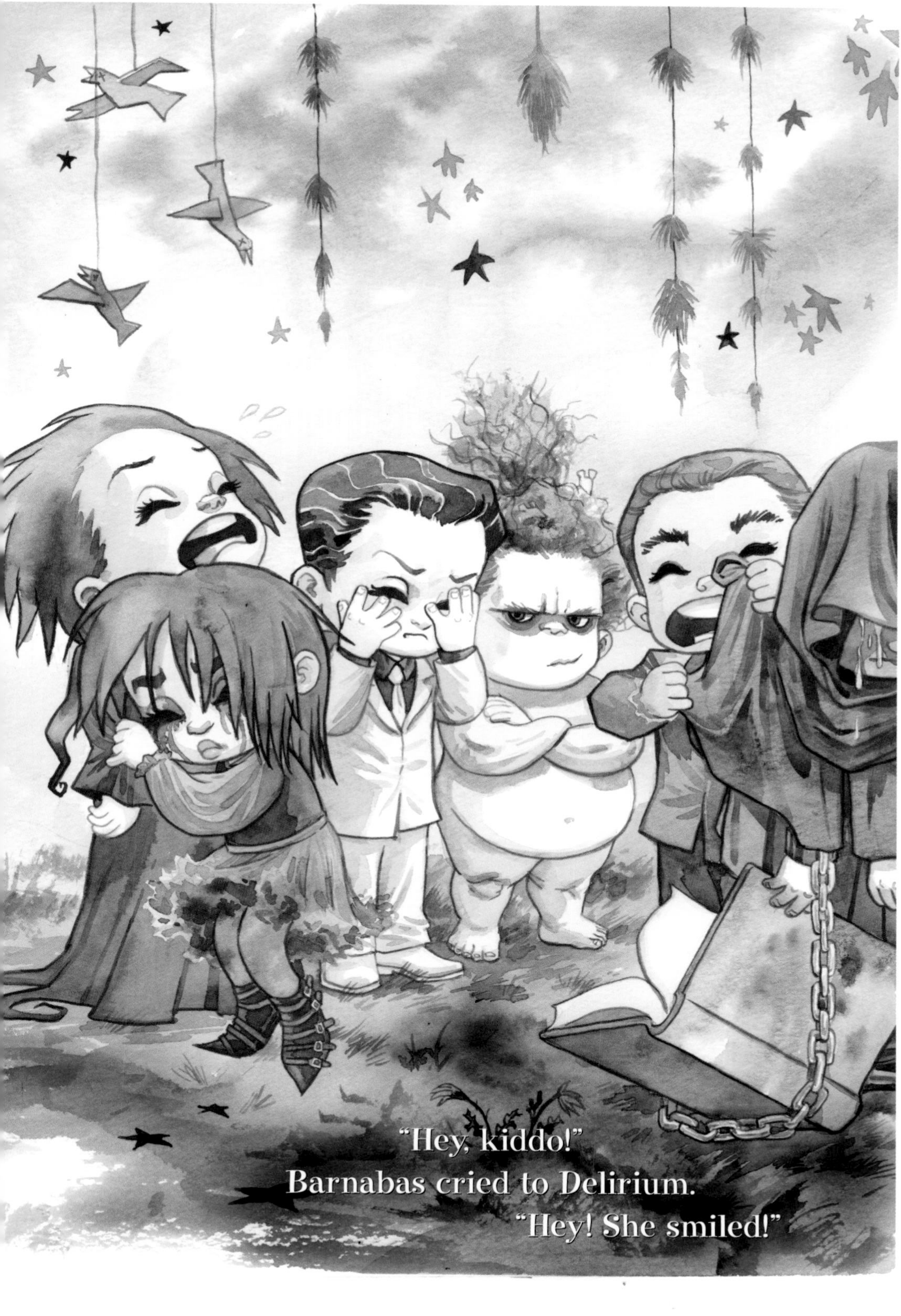

"Hey, kiddo!"
Barnabas cried to Delirium.
"Hey! She smiled!"

"Of course! Everyone's down in the dumps and mopey!
Of course she is smiling! It is a job well done! She is Despair!
It's her job to cause you to feel empty and hopeless and sad!"

And once again, the brights flared, and the floofs flourished,
and the sparkles cracked in the sky.
Delirium danced and the family cheered.
"See, doggie-og-dog! I told you that a party would put a smile
upon her face! I told you! For truly it is the most wonderful thing
in the world to make someone you love smile!"

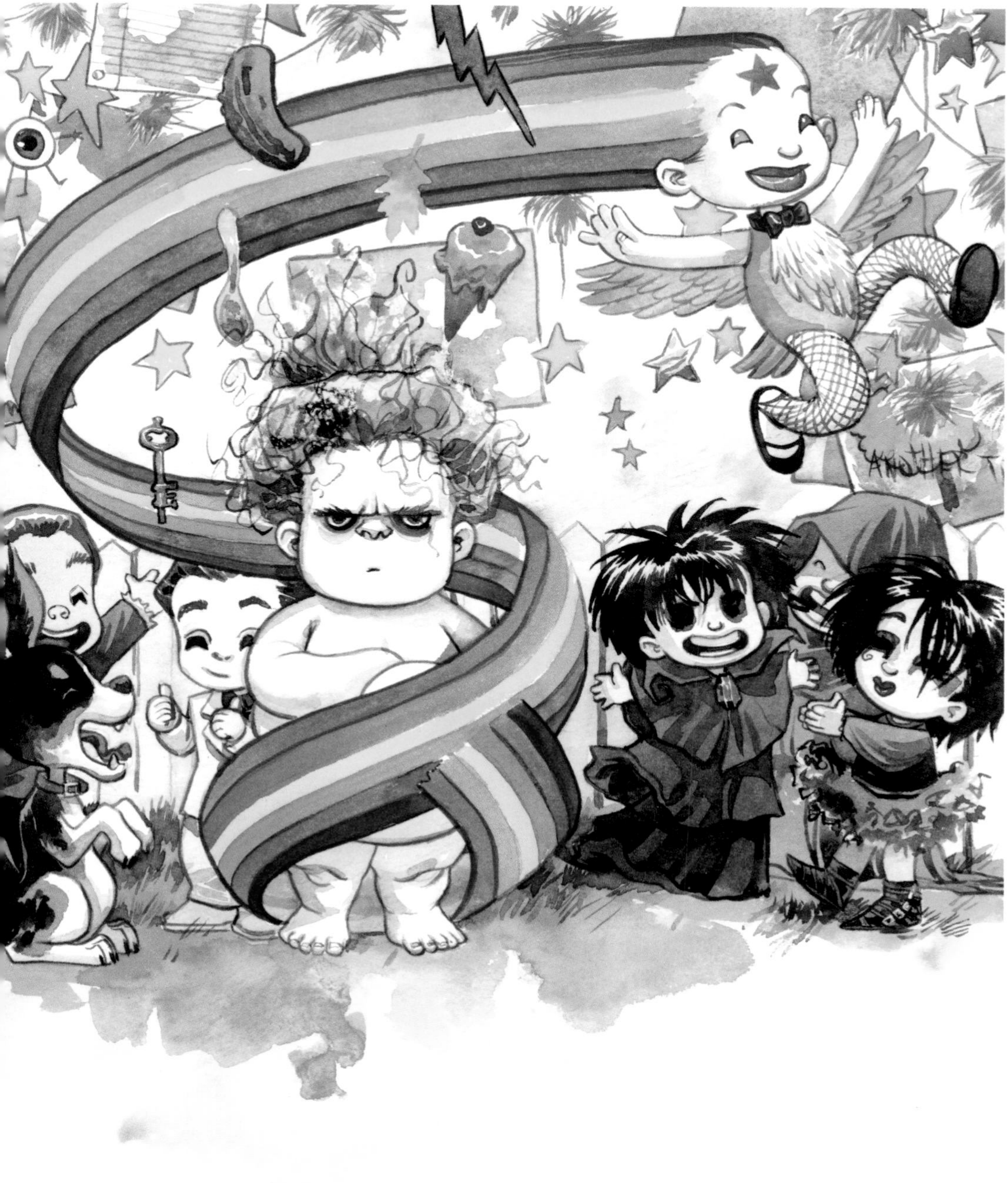

And once again, Despair simply said "..."

The End

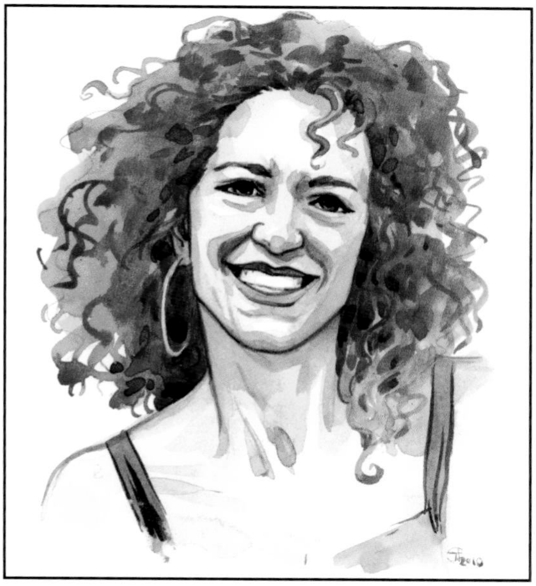

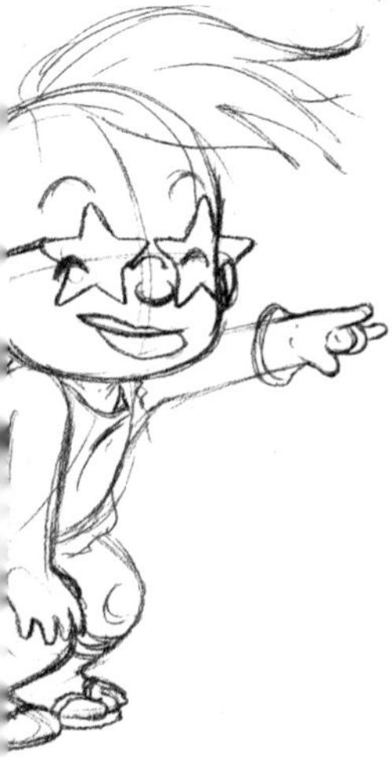

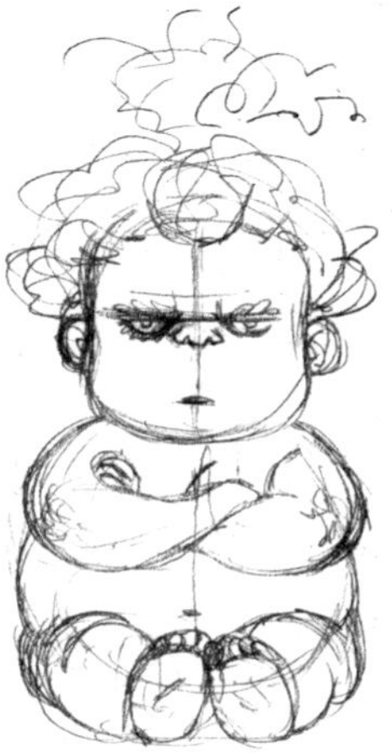

JILL THOMPSON is a comic book illustrator and the creator of *Scary Godmother* and *Magic Trixie*. She's been working in the comic book industry for quite a long time and really, really likes it there. She is a graduate of the American Academy of Art in Chicago. She has been fortunate to win multiple Eisner Awards for her comics work.

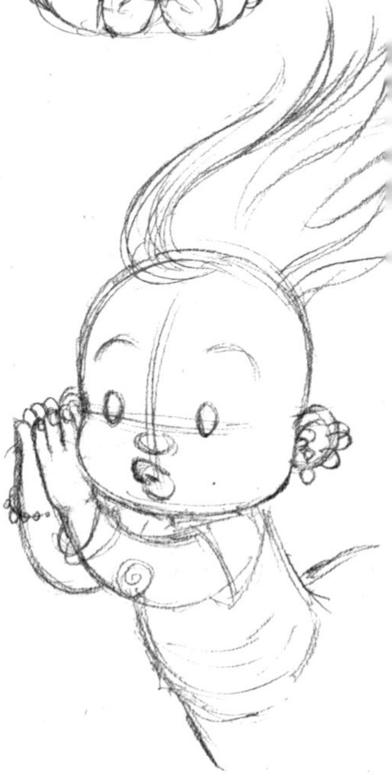

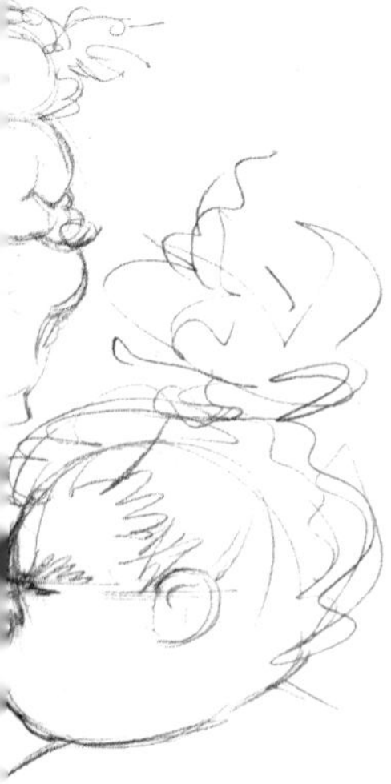

Jill has collaborated with various amazing authors over the years such as Neil Gaiman, Grant Morrison, Will Pfeifer, Evan Dorkin and Mick Foley. If you'd like to check out works other than this fine book by Jill, try these collaborative efforts — *The Sandman: Brief Lives, The Invisibles, Wonder Woman, Finals, Beasts of Burden*, Mick Foley's *Halloween Hijinx* and *Tales from Wrescal Lane*.

For work written and illustrated by Jill and Jill alone, sample Vertigo's *At Death's Door, The Dead Boy Detectives, The Little Endless Storybook* and, of course, the *Scary Godmother* series and *Magic Trixie* series.

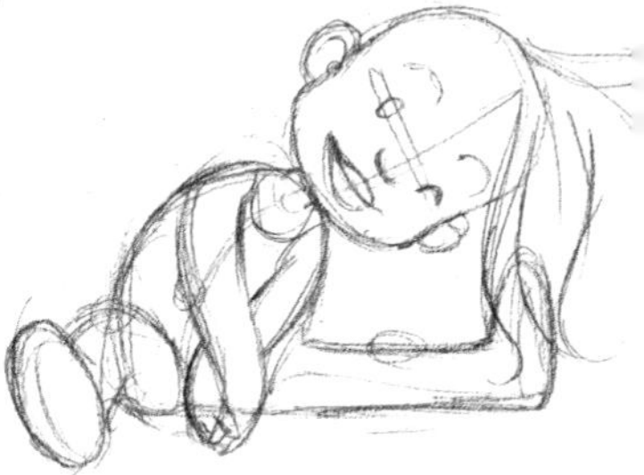

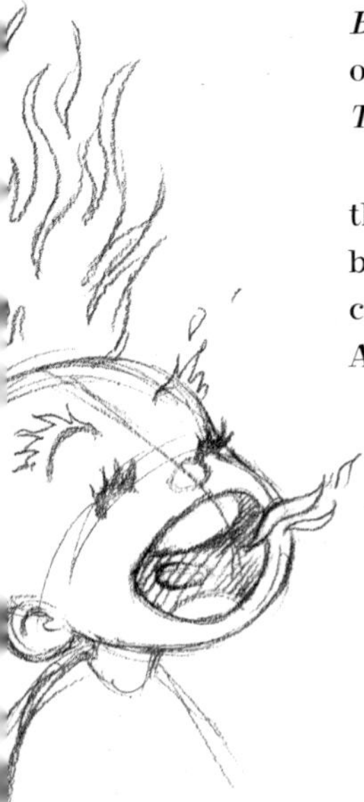

When not creating stories, Jill enjoys making things, cooking stuff, traveling around the US and beyond meeting her fans and speaking about literacy, comics and art. Oh yeah — and having a good time. And smiling. Lots of smiling.

Follow her on Twitter @thejillthompson

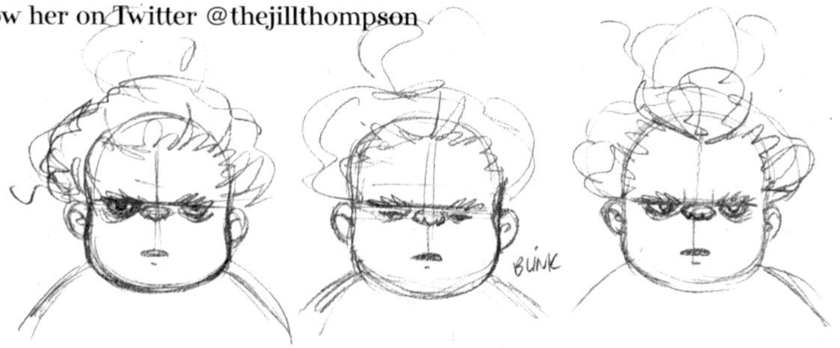
BLINK

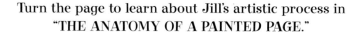

Turn the page to learn about Jill's artistic process in "THE ANATOMY OF A PAINTED PAGE."

This is as detailed as I will pencil for a painting. I do not shade in dark areas unless absolutely necessary. And, I know this page will have a "washed out" feel to it so I wouldn't want there to be any areas with heavy pencil marks showing through. I don't mind a few here and there, because I actually like how that looks, but anything darker would lose the misty feeling I am going for.

I try to erase as much of the superfluous pencil lines to keep it clean, though.

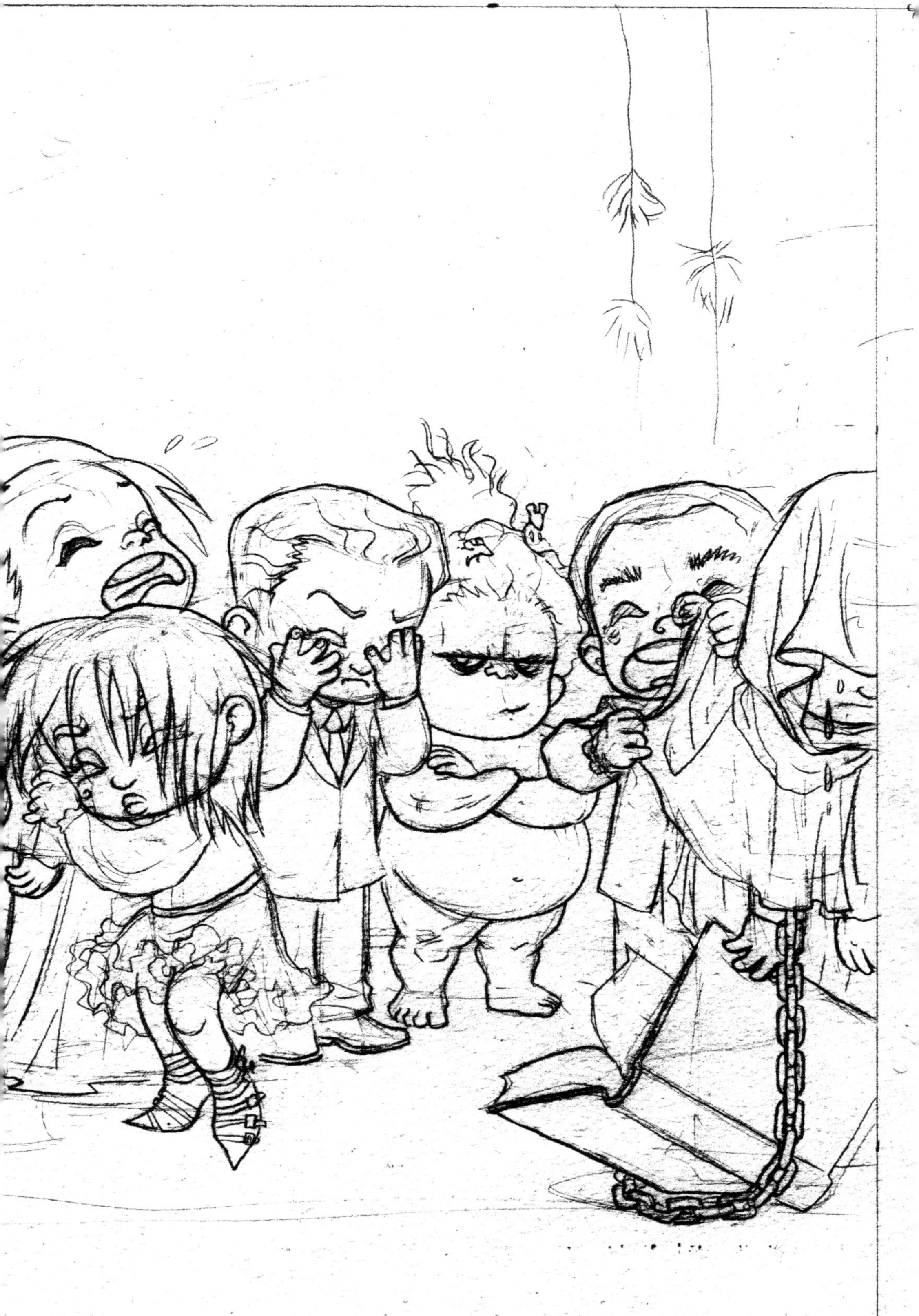

After taping off the panel border to keep a crisp edge, I brush the entire background with water to moisten the page. I work around the figures. I want to keep them crisp. Really, when one works on a painting or illustration with watercolor, it's always best to work from the back (background material) to the front — with your focal point being illustrated at the end. Also, I make sure to establish one of the darkest darks right away, so I know what my value scale is — even if I have to do it on a little scrap of paper and stick it at the edge of the page. Or else things might end up looking flat or washed out, like this page. But that was the whole *object* of this page. But — it's something you should think about when illustrating. So, I let the water absorb a bit: I don't want to have puddles of water on the paper.

Then I begin dropping very thinned-down color in some areas. In others I add much more pigment with each stroke. These will bleed into the wet areas to give the illusion of a foggy or misty environment. I use a little blow dryer to hasten the drying time. But not too much that it will ruin the effect. You gotta play it by ear.

Then I begin adding muted light washes to the characters. In other illos, they would not be muted or this light. But that's what this scene calls for. I add some water to Destiny's book as I put down color so it keeps that misty feeling.

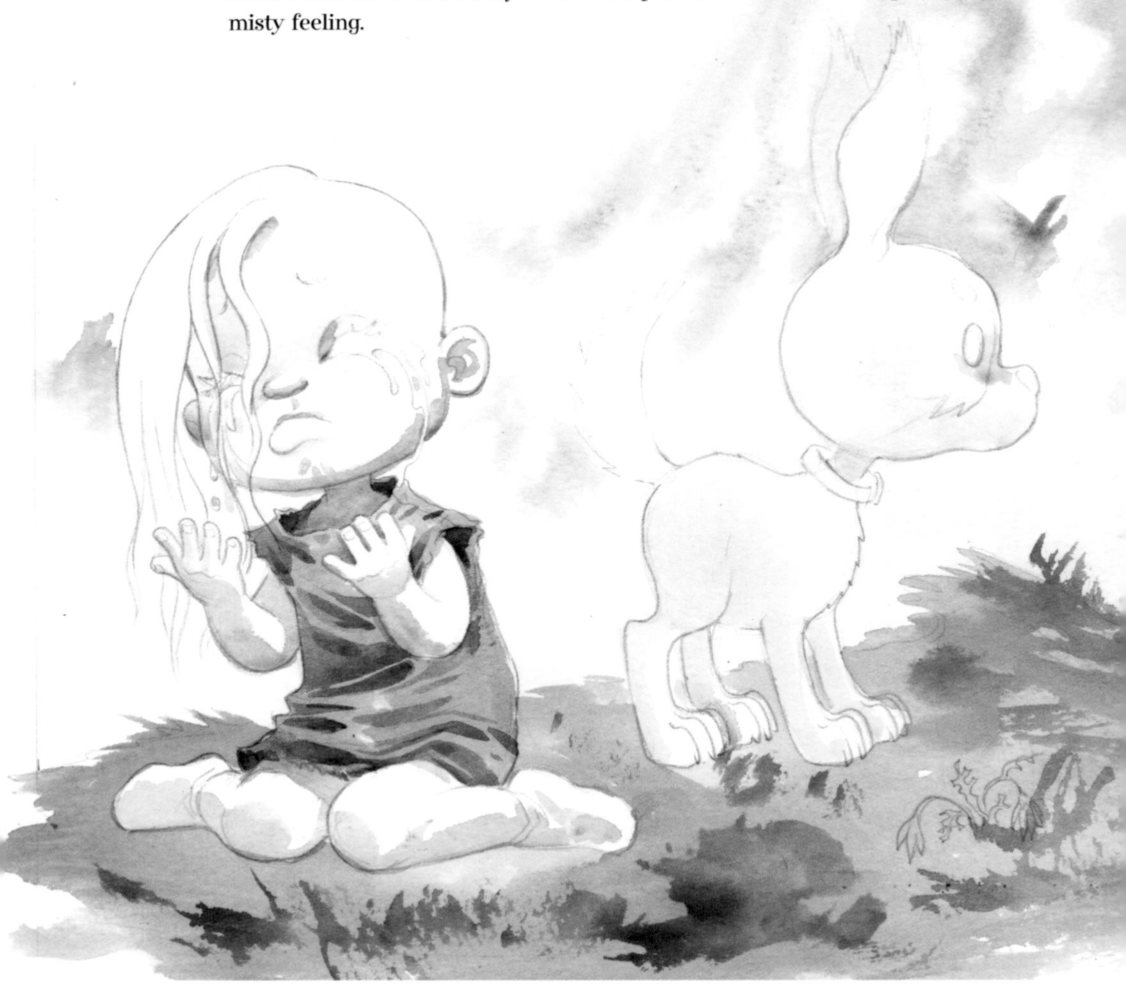

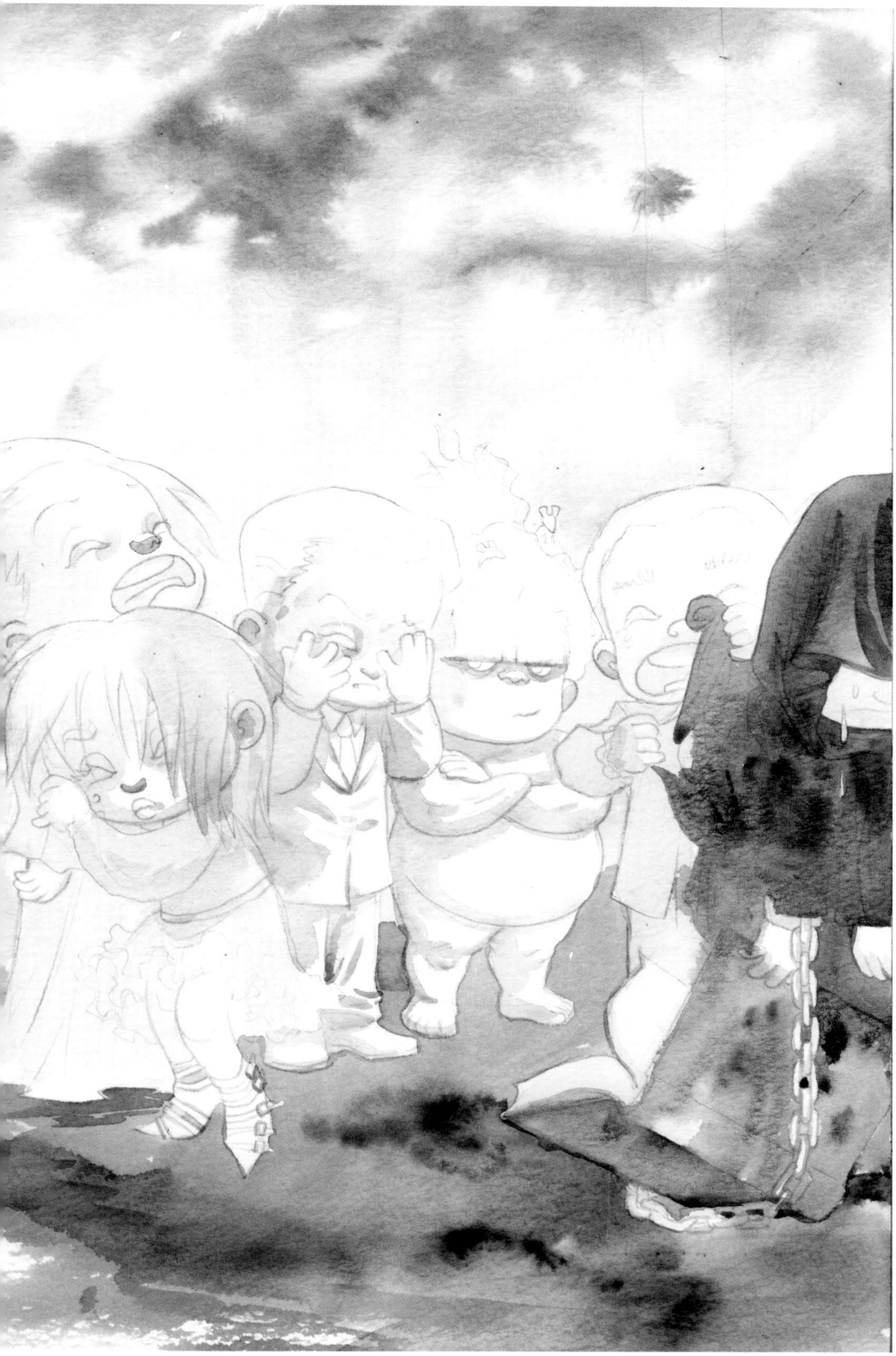

Now I add more color to the characters in the foreground. As things dry, I decide whether or not I want there to be darker values in there. Because this page is supposed to look washed out, I only choose to darken some of the areas that would be filled with darker pigment, like Dream and Death's hair. Usually very saturated and dark, here I liked the watermarks that were created in Death's hair, and the faded quality that Dream had, so I went straight to outlining some of the figures instead of adding shadow which is usually the next step in building the layers of the painting.

I use a number 6-12 brush for my outlining. It's all in watercolor, no inks or dyes. Same stuff as I've used for the bulk of the illustration. After laying down the main colors, then I will go back in and hit things with shadows, delineate things . . . create folds, wrinkles, create planes for hair and face, sculpt things a bit for the finished result.

Flip back to the illustration in this book to see how it turned out.

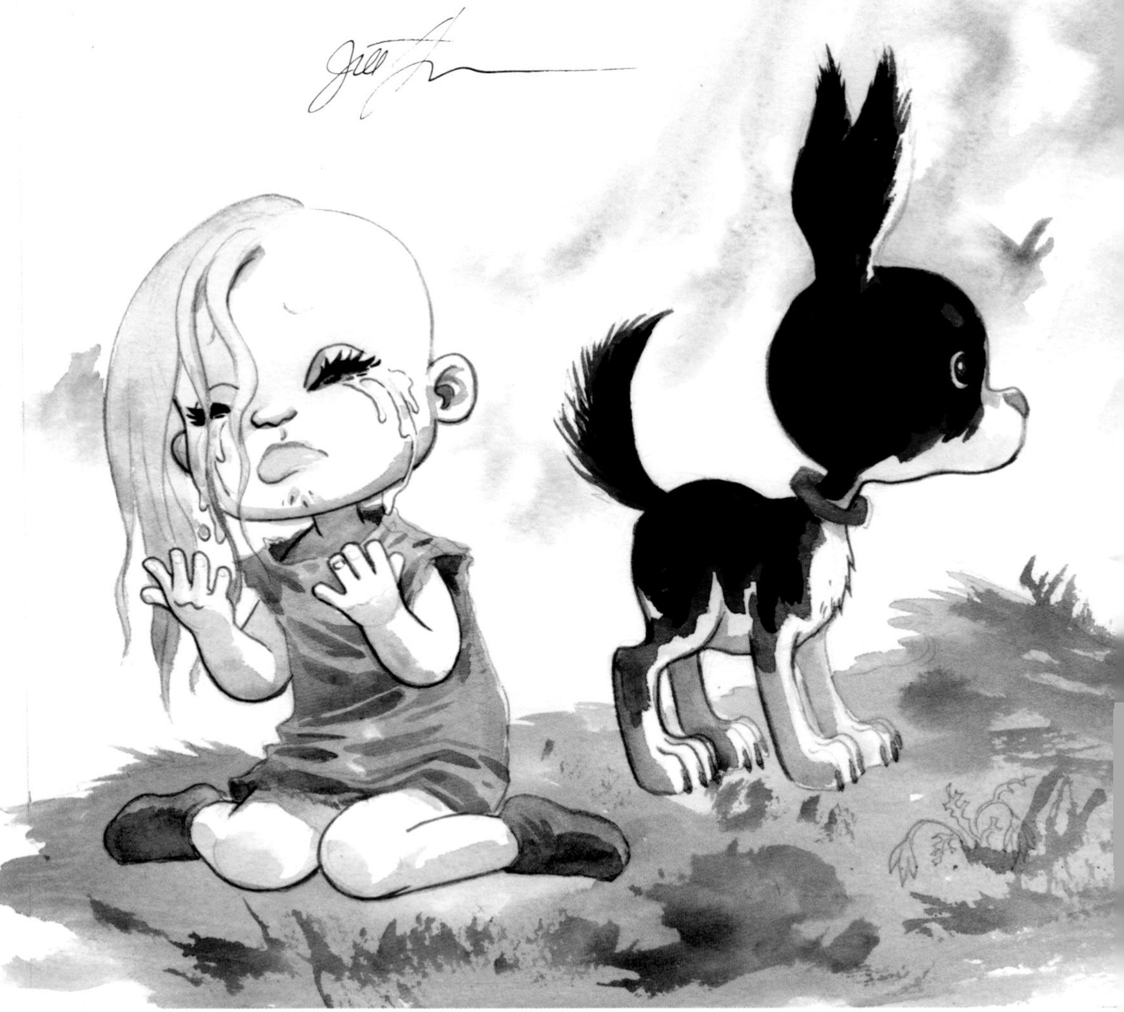

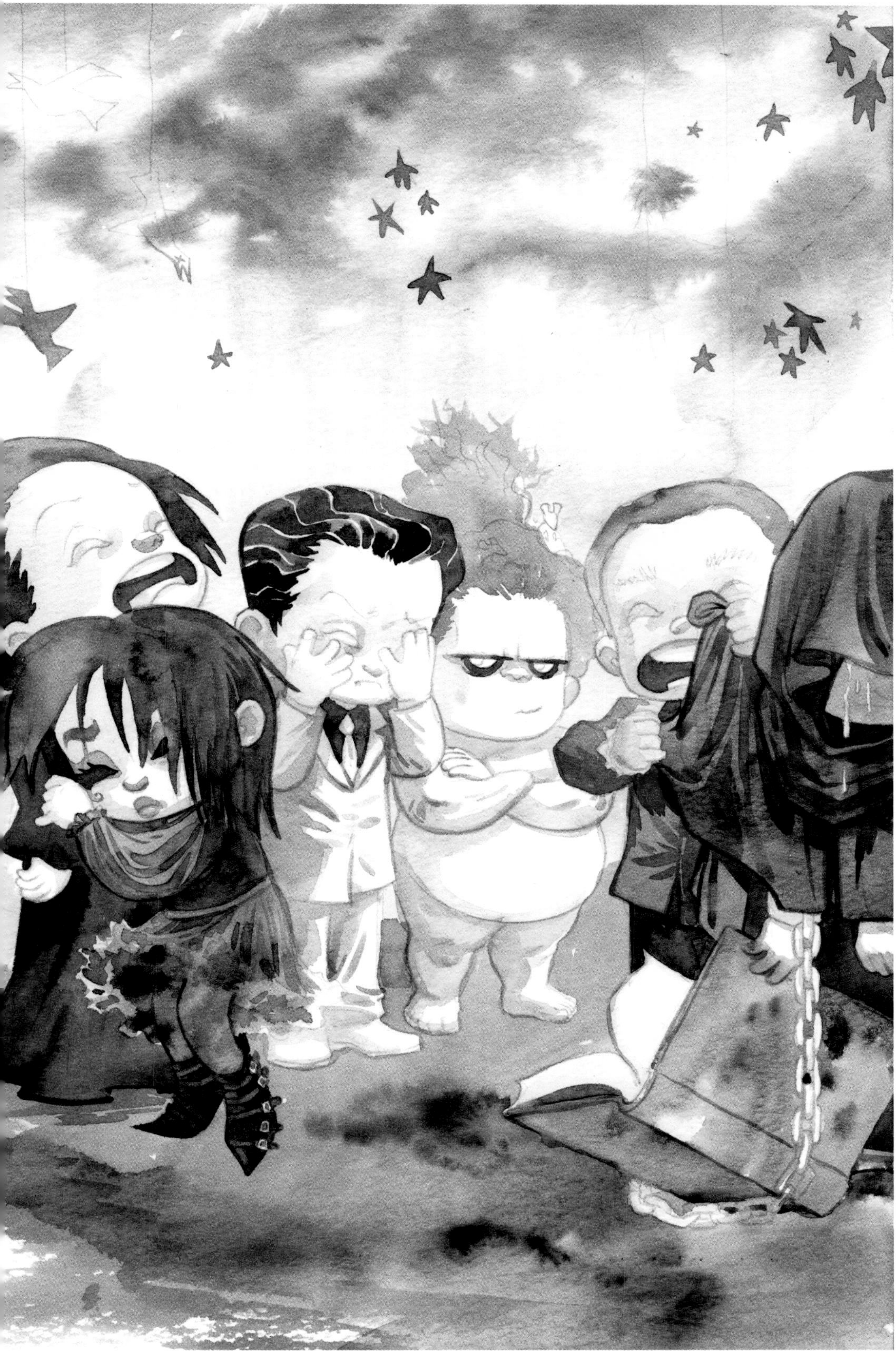

Psst!

If you liked
DELIRIUM'S PARTY,
you'll like

the little ENDLESS storybook

by multiple Eisner award-winning painter

JILL THOMPSON

VERTIGO